*BEETHOVEN'S "ORPHEUS" CONCERTO*

*Ovid empfängt aus den Händen seiner Lieblingsmuse eine Feder, die Sie eben den Fittigen des Amors entrissen hat.*

Engraving by J. Stöber from the chapter "Ovids Leben" in the 1791 Gesellschaft edition of *Ovids Verwandlungen in Kupfern* ("From the hands of his favorite muse, Ovid receives a feather that she just snatched from the wing of Amor." Courtesy of the Ira F. Brilliant Center for Beethoven Studies.

# Beethoven's "Orpheus" Concerto:
# the Fourth Piano Concerto
# in its Cultural Context

OWEN JANDER

*NORTH AMERICAN BEETHOVEN STUDIES NO. 5*

PENDRAGON PRESS
HILLSDALE, N.Y.

NORTH AMERICAN BEETHOVEN STUDIES SERIES
William Meredith, series editor

North American Beethoven Studies is published by Pendragon Press in association
with the American Beethoven Society and The Ira F. Brilliant Center for Beethoven
Studies, San José State University. The first three numbers in the series were
originally published by the University of Nebraska Press and are now available
from Pendragon Press.

1       *Beethoven's Compositional Process*, ed. William Kindermann

2       *Letters to Beethoven and Other Correspondence*, trans. & ed. Theodore Albrecht
        (3 vols.)

3       *The Critical Rception of Beethoven's Compositions by his German Contemporaries*,
        ed. Wayne Senner, Robin Wallace,and William Meredith. (4 vols.) Vols. I and
        II are available.

4       *Transcendent Mastery. Studies in the Music of Beethoven* by Bathia Churgin

5       *Beethoven's "Orpheus" Concerto: the Fourth Piano Concerto in its Cultural
        Context* by Owen Jander

Cover art: Portrait of Beethoven by W. J. Mähler. Courtesy of the Historisches Museum der Stadt Wien.

Library of Congress Cataloging-in-Publication Data

Jander, Owen.
  Beethoven's "Orpheus" concerto : the fourth piano concerto in its cul-
tural context / Owen Jander.
     p. cm. -- (North American Beethoven studies ; no. 5)
  Includes bibliographical references and index.
  ISBN 978-1-57647-132-6
1.  Beethoven, Ludwig van, 1770-1827. Concertos, no. 4, op. 58, piano,
orchestra, G major. 2.  Orpheus (Greek mythology)--Songs and music--
History and criticism. 3.  Program music. 4.  Music and literature.  I. Title.
  ML410.B4J38 2009
  784.2'62--dc22
                                    2008053835

# CONTENTS

# PREFACE

I never realized it at the time, but my involvement with this book began in the spring of 1975 when I first heard the fortepianist Malcolm Bilson play Beethoven's *Sonatas quasi una fantasia*, op. 27, nos. 1-2, at Wellesley College. The instrument he used was a replica of a five-octave Viennese fortepiano, ca. 1795, by the modern builder Philip Belt.

In the summers of the following three years Bilson returned to give fortepiano workshops at Wellesley; for all of us involved in those pioneering adventures with him, they were a matter of constant revelation. So enthusiastic did I become that I commissioned a replica of a six-octave Viennese fortepiano, the sort of instrument that Beethoven would have used in his middle period. Although I am a pianist of limited ability, I discovered that I could perform the *Andante con moto* of Beethoven's Fourth Piano Concerto as a piece for solo piano. (Only much later did I learn that both Fanny Mendelssohn and Franz Liszt were fond of introducing their salon concerts with that engaging musical drama.) As I became more curious about the matter, I encountered Adolph Bernhard Marx's explanation (made back in 1859) that the second movement of Beethoven's Fourth Piano Concerto was elaborately based on the Infernal Scene in Gluck's *Orfeo ed Euridice*. I read the versions of the Orpheus legend by Virgil and Ovid, and one discovery led to the next—countless discoveries!

Over the years I have conducted a lively and helpful correspondence on the subject of Beethoven with Andrew Porter—and an even more animated and helpful correspondence with Warren Kirkendale. From these two scholars I have learned much and I am deeply grateful to them. I am also grateful to a number of people who were (or still are) editors of musical journals and who over the years have accepted articles of mine for publication: Joan Peyser *(The Musical Quarterly)*, William Meredith *(Beethoven Newsletter—later The Beethoven Journal)*, Tilman Seebass *(Imago musicae)*, Walter Frisch *(19th-Century Music)*, Nicholas Kenyon *(Early Music)*, Claudio Annibaldi *(Rivista italiana di musicologia)*, Leon Botstein *(The Musical Quarterly)*, James Hepokoski *(19th-Century Music)*, and Mark Evan Bonds *(Beethoven Forum)*.

As work progressed towards the final stages of this book, four people made much appreciated contributions. Andrew Willis read the text with keen attention and made numerous welcome suggestions. (The most exciting performance of Beethoven's Fourth Piano Concerto I have ever heard was by Andrew Willis, who, not surprisingly, was a student of Malcolm Bilson.) Don Geller, one of the finest technicians in his field, produced the numerous music examples for this book. Claire Brook, the editor of Pendragon Press, has been the godmother of this book, and her associate Bob Kessler has been its admirably efficient factotum.

The world of publishing has always been wary of books about music that include music examples. A retired editor of a press famous for its books about music recently grumbled to me, "Music examples discourage sales." Despite that prejudice, the present book includes more than a hundred examples. Many are brief, but others are not at all brief ... and some extend to three or more pages.

The reader will soon learn that the stories told in this book *require* these examples. My role in this undertaking is to point out details in Beethoven's music that reflect various aspects of the Orpheus legend. The reader can only decide the validity of these relationships, however, if Beethoven's notes are there, on-the-spot.

The numerous music examples in this book pose a problem about which I have become keenly sensitive, this having to do with the layout of a book. Designers of admired books work on the assumption that all pages will have a consistent look. A consistent look is impossible, however, when the most important thoughts set forth in a book are best said by Beethoven's notes. This book will win no prizes for its look—but no lover of Beethoven's Fourth Piano Concerto will complain.

# ABBREVIATIONS

**Anderson**
Anderson, Emily, trans. and ed. *The Letters of Beethoven*, 3 vols. (London: Macmillan. 1961; Reprint, New York: Norton, 1985).

**Beethoven Sketchbooks**
Johnson, Douglas, Alan Tyson, and Robert Winter. *The Beethoven Sketchbooks: History, Reconstruction, Inventory.* Edited by Douglas Johnson. (Berkeley, Ca: University of California Press, 1985).

**Biehl-Naumann**
Naumann, Johann Gottlieb. *Orpheus und Euridice.* Libretto by Charlotte Dorothea Biehl. (Kiel: C. F. Cramer, 1787).

**Brandenburg**
Brandenburg, Sieghard, ed. *Ludwig van Beethoven: Briefwechsel: Gesamtausgabe*, 7 vols. (Munich: G. Henle Verlag, 1996-98).

**Czerny**
Czerny, Carl. *Über den richtigen Vortrag der sämtlichen Beethoven'schen Klavierwerke* (Vienna: A. Diabelli u. Comp. [1842]). Facsimile edited by Paul Badura Skoda. (Vienna: Universal Edition, 1963). Contemporaneous English translation: *On the Proper Performance of All Beethoven's Works for the Piano.* (London, R. Cocks & Co., n.d.). Facsimile edition by Paul Badura-Skoda (Vienna: Universal Edition, 1970).

**Marx**
Marx, Adolf Bernhard. *Ludwig van Beethoven: Leben und Schaffen*, 2 vols. 6th ed. Revised and edited by Gustav Behncke. (Berlin: O. Janke, 1908). The first edition was published in 1859 by Otto Janke; all citations are from the sixth edition.

**Ovid-GE**
*Ovids Verwandlungen in Kupfern, und mit nöthigen Erlauterungen.* 3 vols. Herausgegeben von einer Gesellschaft, 1791.

**Ovid-Loeb**
*Ovid in Six Volumes.* IV: Metamorphoses, with an English translation by Frank Justus Miller. In Two Volumes. II: Books II-XV. (Cambridge, Ma: Harvard University Press, 1916)

**Ovid-Vergil**
*Virgil, with an English Translation by H. Rushton Fairclough.* InTwo Volumes.
    I: Eclogues, Georgics, Aeneid. Rev. ed. Cambridge,Ma.: Harvard
    University Press, 1978.

**Thayer-Forbes**
*Thayer's Life of Beethoven.* Revised and edited by Elliot Forbes. 2 vols.
    Princeton: Princeton University Press, 1964.

**Tovey**
Donald Francis Tovey. *Essays in Musical Analysis.* Vol. 3: *Concertos.*
    London: Oxford University Press, 1936.

# LIST OF FIGURES

*For my companion*


*Gene Cox*


*(who only occasionally understood,*

*but enjoyed the journey,*

*and always trusted)*

# CHAPTER ONE
## *Beethoven's Awareness of the Orpheus Legend*

### BACKGROUND: THE FORCE OF CENSORSHIP THROUGHOUT THE EARLY HISTORY OF PRINTING

Beethoven composed his Fourth Piano Concerto in Vienna in the years 1803-06. In that period there was in Vienna an unusually keen interest in the Orpheus legend, and so it is not surprising to learn that all three movements of the Fourth Piano Concerto were undeclaredly—or better described, secretly—based on that famous story.

This investigation launches with a few brief remarks about the early history of printing and the concomitant role of censorship. The technique of printing books using movable type was invented in the 1430s; the first printed book, of course, was the Gutenberg Bible. One might expect that the Gutenberg Bible would have been followed by a great array of further publications of the Bible. Such was not the case, however, and for the simple reason that for several centuries the Roman Catholic Church strictly forbade the publication of the Bible in vernacular translations. (Their ban was lifted in the nineteenth century; with that reversal of policy, the Bible became the world's most frequently published book.)

### THE JESUIT BAN OF OVID'S *METAMORPHOSES*

Throughout the first four centuries of the history of printing the most frequently published book was Ovid's *Metamorphoses*. The reason was simple: *Metamorphoses* was not only the most elaborate and entertainingly written source of Classical mythology, but was also the best-selling textbook of all time. By the end of the eighteenth century, this monumental work had been published more than a hundred times in London, a hundred times in the French-publishing cities of Europe, and several hundred times in Italy.

In Vienna, however, Ovid's *Metamorphoses* was never published because the work had always been banned. Vienna, capital of the Holy Roman Empire, was notorious for its extremely conservative and suppressive censorship, which was in the hands of a commission of Jesuit professors at the university. To the Jesuit mind, Ovid, author of the *Ars amatoria* and the *Remedia amores*, wrote salacious books, and so all of his works were strictly banned. In Vienna, furthermore, any printer who published a book that had been banned by the Jesuit censors was thrown into prison, his shop closed, and his printing presses destroyed.[1]

---

[1] Anton Mayer, *Wiens Buchdrucker-Geschichte 1482-1882*, 2 vols. (Vienna: W. Frick, 1883-87), 2:109-16.

The Jesuits banned Ovid's *Metamorphoses* because this book frequently dealt with the subject of sex in ways they deemed offensive. Initially offensive were Ovid's many stories having to do with seduction and rape. More offensive were those stories having to do with aberrant sex: incest (e.g., Myrrha, who enlists her nurse in a plot to seduce her own father) and bestiality (e.g., Jupiter, who transforms himself into a bull in order to abduct Europa or into a swan in order to rape Leda). Most offensive to the Jesuit mind, however, were this poet's stories about homosexual love (e.g., Jupiter and Ganymede, Apollo and Hyacinth).

The most abhorrent of all passages in Ovid's *Metamorphoses* was his story about the heroic musician Orpheus, who, having lost his bride Euridice a second time, forswears the love of women, expresses contempt for the sex-obsessed Bacchantes, and goes about singing songs in praise of boys beloved by the gods (again, Ganymede and Hyacinth). Orpheus, according to Ovid, was "the author of Greek love." To the Jesuit mind, no story in Ovid's *Metamorphoses* was more deserving of censorship.

THE GESELLSCHAFT EDITION OF OVID'S *METAMORPHOSES*, VIENNA, 1792

The determined ban of Ovid's *Metamorphoses* by Vienna's Jesuit censors was finally relaxed in 1791 during a period of liberalization.[2] In that year, a society *(Gesellschaft)* founded for this purpose sponsored the publication of a handsome, extensively illustrated, three-volume edition of Ovid in German translation (Fig. 1). The publisher was Ignaz Alberti, who assured the reader  that this edition was "provided with necessary explanations" (mit nöthigen Erläuterungen versehen). These "necessary explanations" were alterations of Ovid's text required by the censors—and they always involved  passages dealing with the subject of sex.

The names of the more than four hundred subscribers to this "Gesellschaft Edition" of 1791 are listed at the beginning of the first volume; this list includes over a dozen people who, over the years, would figure in Beethoven's life. Among the subscribers was Cajetan Giannatasio del Rio, the schoolmaster to whom Beethoven would entrust the education of his nephew. Also listed was Josef Sonnleithner, whom Beethoven would call upon to write the libretto for his opera *Fidelio*. Most important was the young Franz Joseph von Lobkowitz, in whose palace in Vienna Beethoven's Fourth Piano Concerto was first performed in 1807.

(Franz Joseph von Lobkowitz's dates are 1772-1816. When he sponsored the first performance of Beethoven's Fourth Piano Concerto, he was thirty-five years old. He was only nineteen when he subscribed to the Viennese Gesellschaft edition of Ovid's *Metamorphoses* in 1791.)

---

[2] This liberalization is described by Frank T. Brechka, *Gerhard van Swieten and His World, 1700-1772* (The Hague: M. Nijhoff, 1970), 124ff.

**Fig. 1.** Title page of *Ovids Verwandlungen in kupfern und mit den Nöthingen erlaeuterungen. Herausgegeben von einer Gesellschaft* (Vienna, 1791). Courtesy of Houghton Library, Harvard University.

It is clear that Beethoven knew many people in Vienna who not only owned Ovid's *Metamorphoses* but had strong convictions about the value of this work. The introduction in the Gesellschaft edition noted that the German-speaking communities of Europe had long been remiss in their attention to Ovid and expressed the hope that the present publication might serve to correct that problem.

And it did—at least as far as Vienna was concerned. The luxurious Gesellschaft edition was printed simultaneously in an inexpensive version distributed by the publisher Joseph Schalbacher. (At this stage the plates from which the many elegant illustrations in the book were produced were beginning to deteriorate.) Then in the next fifteen years—up to the time Beethoven completed his Fourth Piano Concerto—Ovid's *Metamorphoses* was published in Vienna, in various editions in the original Latin and/or German, six more times.[3] By 1804, the year of the first concert sketches for the concerto, the tales were so well known that a satirical version could be published.[4]

In the years when Beethoven was working on his Fourth Piano Concerto, therefore, he had ready access to Ovid's original Latin text as well as several German translations. These could be purchased in bookshops in Vienna and were found in the private libraries of his patrons.

The year after the Viennese Gesellschaft Edition was published, the twenty-one-year-old Beethoven moved from Bonn to Vienna. By 1792, however, he was already well acquainted with the Orpheus legend and some of the most important music that had been inspired by that legend.

BEETHOVEN'S EARLY ENCOUNTERS WITH THE ORPHEUS LEGEND

The first performance of C. W. Gluck's *Orfeo ed Euridice* took place at the Court Theater in Vienna in 1762—and in the following three decades it would become the most frequently and widely performed opera in Europe.

In 1785 Gluck's *Orfeo* was presented at the Court Theater in Bonn. Beethoven, who was only fourteen years old at the time, would doubtless have experienced this production. It is very likely, in fact, that he was involved in some way with this performance of Gluck's most popular opera.

---

[3] A German translation by August Rode, 1794; a different German translation by J. H. Voss, 1799; the original Latin text, published by J. V. Degen, 1803; a satirical version by Gottlieb Müller, 1804-07 (discussed in the next paragraph here); the Latin text, edited by Fr. X. Schonberger, 1805; and that same edited text, with a simultaneous translation, also in 1805.

[4] Thayer-Forbes, 80.

By this time the prodigiously talented young musician was serving as assistant organist for the court chapel in Bonn. At the same time he was also "cembalist" (i.e., harpsichordist) in the court orchestra. Although it cannot be documented that Beethoven participated in that 1785 production of Gluck's *Orfeo* in Bonn, it is clear that he closely studied both the score and libretto. (In Chapter Two we shall observe how the *Andante con moto* of Beethoven's Fourth Piano Concerto was at several points inspired by the universally-admired Infernal Scene of Gluck's *Orfeo*.)

CRAMER'S PREOCCUPATION WITH ORPHEUS IN HIS *MAGAZIN DER MUSIK* (1782-1787)

During his childhood years in Bonn Beethoven's most influential music mentor was Christian Gottlieb Neefe. In his autobiography Neefe has this to say about his own mentor, Johann Adam Hiller:

> It is this man, then, more than any other, to whom I am indebted in gratitude. He is the well of my better musical knowledge, though I have never been subjected to his teaching in a formal manner. Yet his conversations about musical matters, the suggestions regarding my work, his readiness to supply me with the finest examples, and to point out their most exquisite beauties, as well as the stimulation of further interest by such books as Hume's *Grundsätze der Kritik* and Sulzer's *Theorie,* wherein art was dealt with along psychological lines of thought—all this did more good than any formal instruction might have done.[5]

These lines could equally well describe the relationship between Neefe and his young student Beethoven.

Neefe served as the Bonn correspondent for the *Magazin der Musik,* the most important German music journal of the day. For this journal Neefe submitted two reports describing the musical scene in that city, the first dated December 24, 1782 (pp. 366-68), and the other March 30, 1783 (pp. 377-96). As Neefe concludes this second report, he calls attention to his prodigiously talented student:

> Louis van Beethoven, son of the tenor singer just mentioned, a boy of eleven years,[6] and of most promising talent. He plays the clavier very skillfully and with power, reads at sight very well, and—to put it in a nutshell—he plays chiefly *The Well-Tempered Clavichord* of Sebastian Bach, which Herr Neefe put into his hands. Whoever knows this collection of preludes and fugues in all the keys—which might be called the *non plus ultra* of our art—will know what this means. So far as his duties permitted, Herr Neefe has also given him instruction in thorough-bass. He is now training him in composition and for his encouragement has had nine variations for the pianoforte, written

---

[5] Paul Nettl, *Forgotten Musicians* (New York: Philosophical Library, 1951), 253-54.

[6] At this point Beethoven was in fact twelve years old. Confusion about his exact age continued throughout his entire life.

by him on a march—by Ernst Christoph Dressler—engraved at Mannheim. This youthful genius is deserving of help to enable him to travel. He would surely become a second Wolfgang Amadeus Mozart were he to continue as he has begun.[7]

In his role as Beethoven's mentor, Neefe would doubtless have shared his copies of the *Magazin der Musik* with his young charge of whom he was so proud and supportive.

In the almost five years that the *Magazin der Musik* existed, its founder and editor, Carl Friedrich Cramer, devoted more pages to Orpheus than to any other subject (102 pages, to be precise). This was the result of Cramer's own fascination with the story. He began, on February 21, 1785, with the publication of a German translation of Ranieri Calzabigi's Italian-language libretto of Gluck's *Orfeo ed Euridice*. In an introductory footnote Cramer explained that this translation was the work of Professor Eschenburg in Braunschweig. Cramer expressed his hope that, by publishing Eschenburg's translation, he would promote future performances of Gluck's great opera in German theaters far and wide.

Cramer's enthusiasm for Gluck's *Orfeo* set the stage for his even keener enthusiasm for an Orpheus opera that was premiered in Copenhagen in early 1786. This work, entitled *Orpheus og Euridice*, was the first *opera seria* with a Danish libretto. (Cramer had spent his childhood in Denmark and was fluent in Danish.)

In the chapters ahead there will be many references to this opera. Beethoven owned a copy of the piano-vocal score of the Biehl-Naumann *Orpheus og Euridice*, and the treatment of the Orpheus legend in this opera would have an important influence on Beethoven's Fourth Piano Concerto.

January 28, 1786 (nine pages): Cramer reports his initial impressions of *Orpheus og Euridice* based on his attendance at the dress rehearsal. The libretto of this opera was the work of Charlotte Dorothea Biehl and the score was written by Johann Gottlieb Naumann.

January 30, 1786 (six pages): Cramer reviews the premiere.

December 2, 1786 (one page): Cramer announces a project to publish a piano-vocal score of the Biehl-Naumann *Orpheus und Euridice* and invites subscriptions. (Neefe would be included in the list of subscribers named at the beginning of the published score.)

December 25, 1786 (thirteen pages): Cramer publishes his German translations of the two most important sources of the Orpheus legend, from Virgil's *Georgics* and Ovid's *Metamorphoses*. As a result, when Beethoven was fifteen years old, he already had access to German translations of these basic Latin texts.

---

[7] Thayer-Forbes, 66.

In the same issue (eleven pages): Cramer discusses at length the problems involved in transforming the Orpheus legend into an opera. (Cramer concludes that Dorothea Biehl was more successful than Calzabigi.)

In the same issue (thirty-eight pages), Cramer publishes his German translation of Dorothea Biehl's Danish libretto.

## The satirical treatment of the figure of Orpheus, Vienna, 1787

When Beethoven left Vienna at the end of March 1787 on his first trip to Vienna,[8] he barely missed the Viennese premiere of what became an often-performed musical satire of the Orpheus story, Karl Ditters von Dittersdorf's Die Liebe in Narrenhause (Love in the Insane Asylum) with a libretto by Gottlieb Stephanie the younger.[9] This Singspiel was a satire of Mozart's very successful Die Entführung aus dem Seraglio (Abduction from the Harem), for which Stephanie had written the libretto five years earlier. The satire was premiered at the Kärntnerthortheater on April 12, 1787; five performances followed that month, and it moved to the Burgtheater in July. The setting of an asylum would have been amusing for its audience, since Emperor Joseph II had just established in Vienna one of Europe's first insane asylums. On weekends the public could buy tickets so they could gape at the inmates restrained in cages.

Stephanie's cast of characters is based on the familiar Mozart Singspiel: Bassa Selim (Mozart) becomes Bast (Dittersdorf); Blondchen becomes Clärchen; Belmonte becomes Albert—while Constanza remains Constanza. The character Pedrillo in Die Entführung becomes a caricature of the composer Dittersdorf called Orpheus in Die Liebe im Narrenhause. Orpheus has come to the insane asylum to rescue his Euridice—who is Clärchen. He poses as an inmate of the asylum, managing to persuade people that he is crazy by "talking" to them with his violin.

This joke would have delighted the Viennese audience in 1787 since it involved an allusion they would have been quick to catch. Dittersdorf, himself a famous violinist, had created a sensation four years earlier at the popular concerts in the Augarten with his programmatic symphonies based on mythological stories from Ovid's Metamorphoses. In the symphony that tells the story of Leto and the Lycian peasants, Dittersdorf had used his violin to imitate the speech of frogs, engendering a reaction that was a mixture of amazement, amusement, and outrage.[10] This becomes the subject of a curious subplot in Die Liebe im Narrenhause, introduced by this encounter:

[8] Dieter Haberl, "Beethovens erste Reise nach Wien—Die Datierung seiner Schülerreise zu W. A. Mozart," Neues Musikwissenschaftliches Jarhbuch 14 (2006): 215-55.

[8] A more elaborate version of the following discussion is found in my "The 'Kreutzer' Sonata as Dialogue," Early Music 16, no. 1 (Feb. 1988), 34-49, esp. 45-47.

[10] Eduard Hanslick, Geschichte des Concertwesens in Wien (Vienna: W. Braumüller, 1869), iii.

Act I, scene 10
*Bast, Trübe, and Orpheus*

*Orpheus: (enters, making appealing facial expressions, steps between Bast and Trübe and plays on his violin)*

*Bast: (to Orpheus)* Very well, thank you. And you? Did you also sleep well? (Orpheus continues to play his violin, and exits.)

*Trübe: (laughing)* What was *that* all about?

*Bast:* That fellow is a fine violinist who is so enamoured with his own playing that he's become a bit crazy on the subject. He imagines that he can express his thoughts through his violin playing; therefore he almost never talks. Just now he came and wished me good morning and asked whether I had slept well; then, in response to my own question, he replied that he himself had not slept well on account of a headache.

*Trübe:* In my whole life I have never heard of anything like that.

*Bast:* As a result of this he imagines that he is the famous musician Orpheus, who overwhelmed the devils with his music. Otherwise he is very well behaved, gets in no one's way, and so is permitted to go about freely.

*Trübe:* Ha! Ha! Ha!

This curious subplot is then pursued in Scene 16 where Orpheus appears with Clärchen, and Constanze with Albert.

*Orpheus: (approaches Clärchen with intense and adoring expression, playing his violin)*

*Clärchen*: That's wonderful, Monsieur Orpheus!

*Orpheus:* Then you appreciate what my bow is saying? You understand the thoughts I am trying to express?

*Constanze and Albert: (whisper secretly to one another)*

*Clärchen:* Every syllable! One needs only to have sensibility.

*Orpheus:* That's it, Mademoiselle! One must feel; one must sympathize with the emotions; then one understands me indeed. For whenever I wish to express a thought, it travels like a bolt of lighning from my head to my heart, and from my heart to the tips of my fingers. When my fingers set the bow and the strings in motion, that thought is communicated in full strength through the rubbing of the bow on the strings to the notes I draw forth. Whoever possesses keen sensibility [ein feines Gefühl], that person is immediately electrified by these notes, and senses in his own heart the expression of my thoughts.

*Clärchen:* You are right, Monsieur Orpheus. That's exactly how it happens with me. When I hear you make music it is as though someone had written your thoughts right into my heart.

*Orpheus:* However, one must have keen sensibility. Otherwise how would it have been possible for me, without the use of magic, to have ventured into the Underworld as I did in search of Euridice?

*Clärchen:* But what are you telling us, Monsieur Orpheus? And did the infernal spirits not harm you?

*Orpheus:* Harm *me*? Ha! Ha! Ha! With a single stroke of my bow I captured them. They beat their breasts, were melted to tears by my sensitive playing, and Pluto threw himself at my feet like a Polish dog. But one must have keen sensibility.

*Clärchen:* If you could move even the devils—

*Orpheus:* Believe me, the devils are often much sooner moved than many human beings. There are a great many thick-eared creatures—especially among human beings—on whom not even a braying trombone can make an impression.

*Clärchen:* That I well believe.

*Orpheus:* That's because you have keen sensibility. I assure you, I have not yet met another person on whom I have made such an impression as I have on you.

SONG

Therefore I am drawn to you
because the stroke of my bow
excites such emotion in you.

(*Before each of these three lines, he plays on his violin with the tenderest facial expressions as though the text of the song were to explain what he had first said with his music.*)

In contrast, there are those
who through neither laughter or tears
can be moved to involvement.

(END OF SCENE)

(See Fig. 2 on p. 10)

Silly as these scenes are, they indicate the delight taken by audiences in Beethoven's time with the artifice of a composer "saying" things with textless instrumental music.

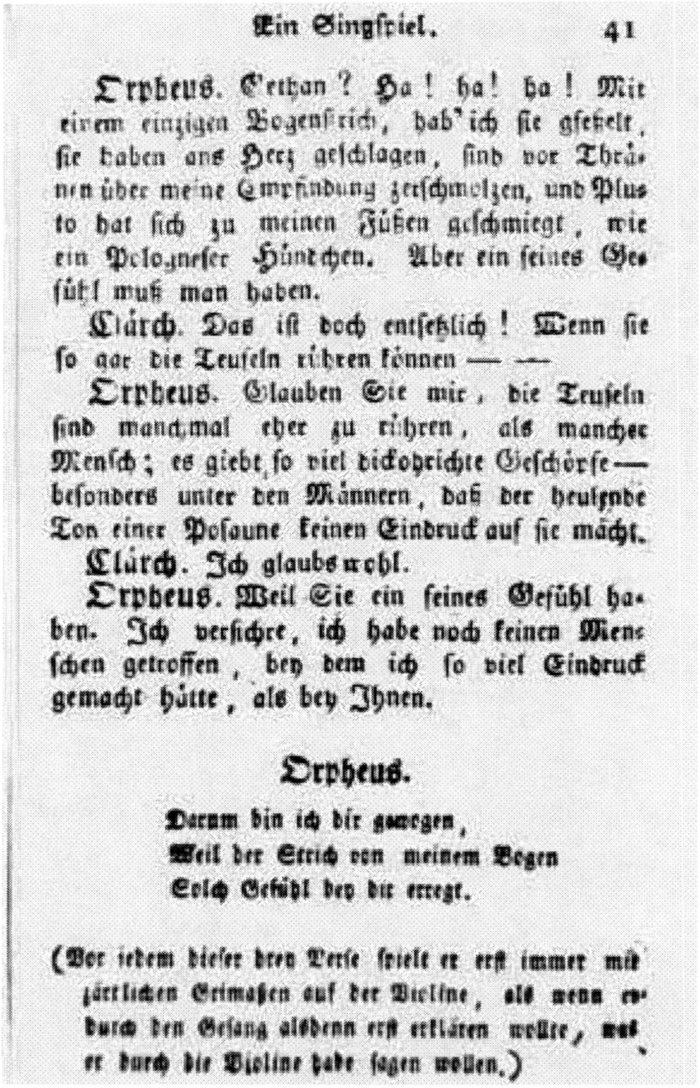

Ein Singspiel.                          41

Orpheus. Erthan? Ha! ha! ha! Mit einem einzigen Bogenstrich, hab' ich sie gsehelt, sie haben ans Herz geschlagen, sind vor Thränen über meine Empfindung zerschmolzen, und Pluto hat sich zu meinen Füßen geschmiegt, wie ein Pelognefer Hündchen. Aber ein feines Gefühl muß man haben.

Clärch. Das ist doch entsetzlich! Wenn sie so gar die Teufeln rühren können — —

Orpheus. Glauben Sie mir, die Teufeln sind manchmal eher zu rühren, als mancher Mensch; es giebt, so viel dickohrichte Geschörfe — besonders unter den Männern, daß der heutende Ton einer Posaune keinen Eindruck auf sie macht.

Clärch. Ich glaubs wohl.

Orpheus. Weil Sie ein feines Gefühl haben. Ich versichre, ich habe noch keinen Menschen getroffen, bey dem ich so viel Eindruck gemacht hätte, als bey Ihnen.

### Orpheus.

Darum bin ich dir gewogen,
Weil der Strich von meinem Bogen
Solch Gefühl bey dir erregt.

(Vor jedem dieser drey Verse spielt er erst immer mit zärtlichen Grimasen auf der Violine, als wenn er durch den Gesang alsdann erst erklären wollte, was er durch die Violine habe sagen wollen.)

**Fig. 2.** Stephanie-Dittersdorf. *Die Liebe im Narrenhause*. (Vienna: April 1787), page 41.

The great success of *Die Liebe in Narrenhause* is clear from its frequent performances outside Vienna in the following decades. The year after its Viennese premiere, the work was presented in Hamburg in an adaptation of music and text entitled *Orpheus der Zweyte* (Orpheus the Second);

performances of the original version were given in Frankfurt in 1788; Hanover in 1789; Stuttgart, Munich, and Budapest in 1790; Berlin in 1791; Liegnitz and Amsterdam in 1792; and Warsaw in 1793; and the work was revived in Frankfurt in 1793, Stuttgart in 1808, and in Würzburg in 1813.[11] As Thomas Baumann noted, "... Dittersdorf's music ensured the opera's popularity on nearly all German operatic stages."[12]

The vogue for textless instrumental dialogue satirized by Stephanie in 1787 was, fifteen years later, incorporated by Beethoven into a work of supreme art. Two months after this work was published, in a brief announcement in the *Allgemeine musikalische Zeitung*, it was described in the following manner—and this description can only have been Beethoven's own:

> Dedicated to the famous Kreutzer in Paris, this sonata requires for its performance two artists who are in very mighty command of their instruments, and who understand how to use them with meaning and with feeling [mit Sinn und Gefühl]. One finds here not just a random murmuring with notes; rather, one believes that one perceives a penetrating dialogue, relentlessly driven forward, which sets and maintains our imagination and sensitivity in motion.[13]

The "penetrating dialogue" is launched in the slow introduction of the first movement, where the violinist and the pianist—without text—discuss the importance of the iambic gesture "up-down." This gesture will then serve as a unifying obsession flowing through all three movements of Beethoven's "Kreutzer" Sonata. (The "Kreutzer" Sonata was Beethoven's maiden voyage in cyclic organization.)[14]

### MÜLLER'S SATIRE OF OVID'S *METAMORPHOSES*, VIENNA, 1804-1807

During the years 1804 to 1807, the Viennese enthusiasm for Ovid led to the publication of a satirical version of his *Metamorphoses* by an obscure but impressively skilled poet named Gottlieb Müller: *Ovids Verwandlungen travestiert* was issued in a series of pocket-size volumes that were sold to the fun-loving patrons of Vienna's coffee houses and wine gardens. Müller delivered Ovid's narratives in a virtuosic outpouring of seven-line stanzas (hundreds of them!) that are energized by a constant poetic rhythm: four lines, followed by three lines. (The first four lines are the set-up; the following

---

[11] Alfred Loewemberg, *Annals of Opera 1597-1940*, 3rd. ed. (London: John Calder, 1978), 442.
[12] *New Grove Dictionary of Opera*, s.v. "*Die Liebe in Narrenhaaus*," 2:1257.
[13] See my "The 'Kreutzer' Sonata as Dialogue," 34-35.
[14] *Ibid.*, 45.

three lines deliver the joke.) A recurring delight of Müller's travesty is the way it pokes fun at the foibles of Viennese society of the day.

By amusing coincidence, Müller's satirical versions of Books 10 and 11 in Ovid's *Metamorphoses* (the two books that contain the Orpheus legend) were published together in a single volume in 1807—the same year as the first performance of Beethoven's Fourth Piano Concerto (Fig. 3). This publication, it must be declared at the outset, had no influence on Beethoven's concerto. It is merely a fascinating example of the "Orpheus rage" in Vienna in those years.

Of particular interest in Müller's treatment of the Infernal Scene in the Orpheus tale are two events. On page 10 of Müller's booklet we find these two stanzas:

> Wo Satan seine Knisse nicht
> vermögend auszuführen,
> da schickt er, sagt ein alt Gedicht,
> ein Weib, zu spioniren.
>     So war's auch hier, der Dichter schaut*)
> begierig um nach seiner Braut,
> die blieb im Kothe stecken.
>
> Vergeblich rief er: Sapperment!
> das Weib sank immer tiefer,
> vergeblich rang er seine Händ'
> nur leere Luft ergriff er.**)
>     J[e]tzt wollt' er zu der Alten hin.
> Die lief, und denkt in ihrem Sinn:
> Leb wohl, du dummer Laffe.
>
> Where Satan was no longer able
> to carry out his intrigues,
> according to an ancient poem,
> he sent a woman to spy.
>     And so it was here, the poet*)
> eagerly turned around to look at his wife,
> who now got stuck in the mud.
>
> In vain he cried out "Sapperment"!
> [a euphemism for "Sacramento!," a cussword of the day]
> The woman sank ever deeper,
> in vain he wrung his hands,
> but grasped only empty air.**)
>     Now he wants to go out after his old lady.
> She ran off, and thought to herself,
> So long, you dumb fop.

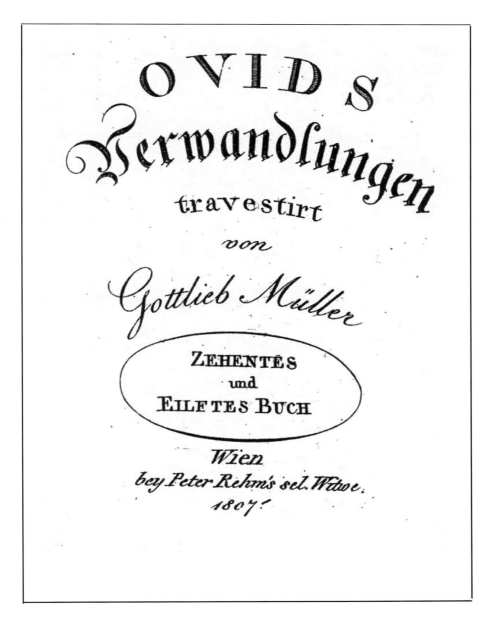

**Fig. 3.** Title page of *Ovids Verwandlungen Travestiert von Gottlieb Müller*. Books 10 and 11 (Vienna, 1807). Courtesy of the Museum der Volskünde, Vienna.

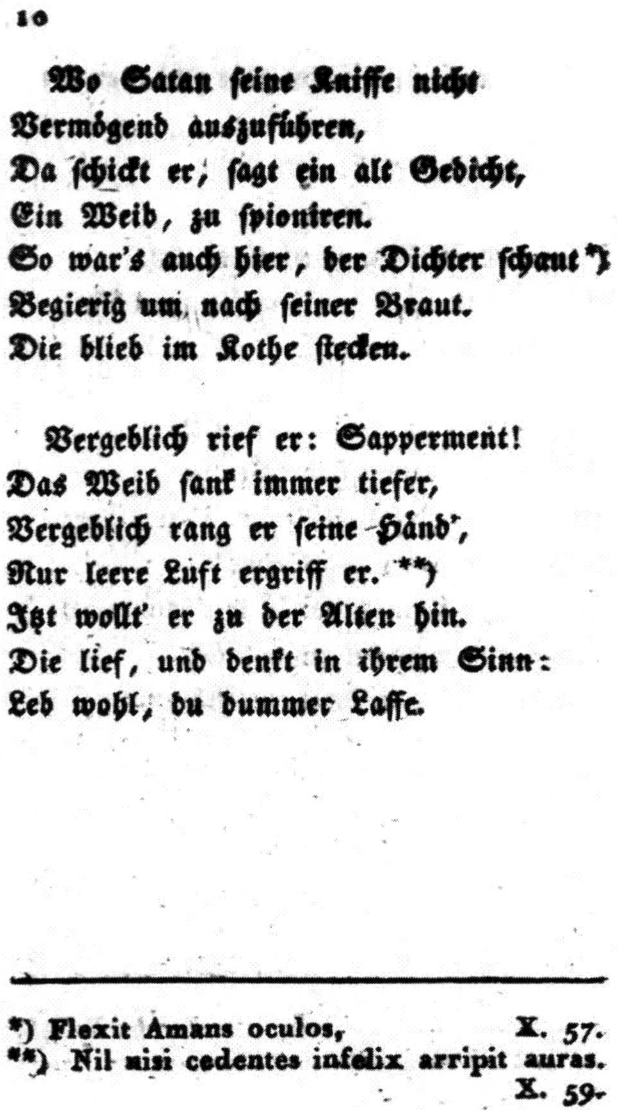

10

Wo Satan seine Kniffe nicht
Vermögend auszuführen,
Da schickt er, sagt ein alt Gedicht,
Ein Weib, zu spioniren.
So war's auch hier, der Dichter schaut *)
Begierig um, nach seiner Braut.
Die blieb im Kothe stecken.


Vergeblich rief er: Sapperment!
Das Weib sank immer tiefer,
Vergeblich rang er seine Händ',
Nur leere Luft ergriff er. **)
Itzt wollt' er zu der Alten hin,
Die lief, und denkt in ihrem Sinn:
Leb wohl, du dummer Laffe.

---

*) Flexit Amans oculos,                                    X. 57.
**) Nil nisi cedentes infelix arripit auras.
                                                            X. 59.

**Fig. 4.** *Ovids Verwandlungen travestiert von Gottlieb Müller,* BOOKS 10 AND 11
(VIENNA, 1807), PAGE 10. Courtesy of the Museum der Volkskunde, Vienna.

There are two lines in Müller's treatment of the story of Orpheus in Hades
that were of such interest to the satirist that he fitted these lines with
footnotes quoting Ovid. (Many purchasers of these volumes had learned
their Latin by translating stories from *Metamorphoses*.) These two lines had
been of equal interest to Beethoven.

Müller's first footnote, "Flexit Amans oculos," reports that most famous of all moments in the Orpheus legend where the heroic love breaks his vow. "The lover turns his eyes" to look upon Euridice ... whereupon she vanishes into the darkness. (The satirist's version is "So war's auch hier, der Dichter schaut / Begierig um nach seiner Braut.")

In Beethoven's *Andante con moto* this gripping moment occurs in measure 55 and is extended through measure 61.

Müller's other footnote is "Nil nisi cedentes infelix arripit auras." Here Ovid decribes Orpheus's desperate attempt to reach for Euridice and draw her back. "Unhappy man, he grasped only the empty air." (The satirist's version is "Vergeblich rang er seine Händ' / Nur leere Luft ergriff er.")

In Beethoven's *Andante con moto* this gesture occurs in the very last measure. These two coincidences are easily explained. These are the most dramatic and graphically suggestive events in Ovid's account of this famous scene—and in the next chapter of this book I shall return to these two passages in their context.

KANNE'S *ORPHEUS*, VIENNA, **1807**

Another example of the interest in the Orpheus legend in Vienna in the year of the first performance of Beethoven's Fourth Piano Concerto is a two-act opera titled *Orpheus* premiered in the Court Theater in 1807. Both the libretto and score of this opera were the work of Friedrich August Kanne, who was a close friend of Beethoven (see Fig. 5).

The opening lines of the first-act finale of Kanne's *Orpheus* has a sequence of arresting relationships to the opening phrases of the second movement of Beethoven's Fourth Piano Concerto. In the next chapter of this book I shall examine how these arresting relationships come about.

THE PARIS EDITION OF OVID'S *METAMORPHOSES* **(1767-1771)**, AND ITS FAMOUS ILLUSTRATIONS OF THE ORPHEUS LEGEND

The Viennese Gesellschaft Edition of 1791—so important to our present investigation—was inspired by a sumptuous four-volume set of Ovid's *Metamorphoses* created in Paris between 1767 and 1771. Four volumes were required because it included both Ovid's Latin text and a Jesuit-approved French translation. The eighteenth-century French edition stands as the most luxurious publication of the *Metamorphoses* in the entire history of printing. The expensive enterprise was made possible through financing provided by a consortium of ten publishers, each of whom received an equal share of copies. Each publisher then sold these sets of four books in his own handsome, distinctive bindings, supplying his own title pages.[15]

---

[15] Harvard University's Houghton Library owns four of these sets—by the publishing houses of Pissot, Despilly, Prault, and Le Clerc. Apart from their bindings and title pages, the four sets are identical.

18                          Orpheus.

(Unter dem stärksten Donner stürzen die Felsen ein, und
man ficht den Eingang in die Unterwelt, aus dem meh-
rere Larven mit Flambeaus hervortreten.)


## Dreyzehnte Scene.

### Orpheus und Chor der Geister.

#### Finale.

Orpheus.

Ich wandle froh die Schreckensbahn

Chor.

Ha! wer wagt es hier zu nah'n!

Orpheus.

Ich suche meines Lebens Glück.

Chor.

Ha! Verwegner geh zurück.

Orpheus.

Ihr Saiten rauscht im hellen Chor,

Chor.

Du betäubst nicht unser Ohr.

Orpheus.

Eröffnet mir das dunkle Thor,

Chor.

Nimmer öffnet sich dieß Thor,
Du bringst mit keiner Macht
In Orkus finstre Nacht.

Orpheus.

Ich bebe nicht vor Orkus Nacht,
Mich schützt der Töne Zaubermacht,

Fig. 5. Title page of the libretto of Kanne's *Orpheus, eine grosse Oper in zwei Aufzügen*
(Vienna: 1807).

What made this sumptuous edition valuable (and expensive) was the inclusion of 140 elegant illustrations by an array of distinguished artists, among them no less a figure than François Boucher.[16] The 140 illustrations were then reproduced as engravings created by a team of the most skilled artisans in Paris. Wealthy families used these beautiful illustrations to guide their children through the world of Classical mythology.

A very limited number of copies of these 140 engravings to be drawn from the plates were issued by themselves in a separate edition, without Ovid's text: *Les Métamorphoses d'Ovid gravées sur les desseins des meilleurs peintres français. Par les soins des s.rs Le Mire et Basans, graveurs.* This edition was dedicated to the Duke of Chartres,[17] and these volumes were bound with breath-taking elegance (see Fig. 6).

In the Viennese Gesellschaft edition of Ovid's *Metamorphoses* (1791), the 140 illustrations from the Paris edition were copied—in modern terms, *pirated*—by a team of local engravers who substituted German captions for the original French captions. As in the Paris original, the illustrations leap out as the most engaging feature of the Viennese publication.

The inclusion of the foregoing bibliographical information is to call the reader's attention to the fact that five of these illustrations—those having to do with the Orpheus legend—find specific musical reflection at important moments in Beethoven's Fourth Piano Concerto. Here is the sequence in which these five plates occur in the Paris and Vienna editions:

1. Orpheus, leading Euridice out of Hades, breaks his vow and turns to look at his bride. (Fig. 10 on p. 38). In Beethoven's score, the second movement, mm. 55-56.

2. Orpheus, playing his lyre, enchants all of nature (Fig. 12 on p. 58). In Beethoven's score, the first movement, mm. 1-5 and 6-14.

3. Jupiter, in the form of an eagle, carries Ganymede to Mount Olympus (Fig. 13 on p. 77). In Beethoven's score, the first movement, mm. 105-111.

4. Apollo laments the death of Hyacinth, who has been struck dead by a discus thrown by Apollo (Fig. 14 on p. 78). In Beethoven's score, the first movement, mm. 119-123.

5. The Bacchantes attack Orpheus and destroy him (Fig. 16 on p. 123). In Beethoven's score, the third movement, mm. 32ff.

---

[16] Several of the illustrations of the Orpheus legend were by the painter Jean-Michel Moreau "le jeune" (1741-1814), who was later appointed "Dessinateur des Menus-Plaisirs du Roi" ("Illustrator of the Festivities and Ceremonies of the King [Louis XV, and then Louis XVI]").

[17] The Duke of Chartres was Louis Philippe Joseph (1747-93), who was caught up in the liberal Enlightenment movements of his day, and later became known as "Philippe-Égalité." Harvard also owns a copy of this extremely luxurious volume.

**Fig. 6.** Title page of *Les Métamorphoses d'Ovide gravées sur les desseins des Meilleurs Peintres Français* (Paris: Le Mire et Bassans [1770]). Courtesy of the Department of Printing and Graphic Arts, Houghton Library, Harvard College Library.

At appropriate points in the following three chapters I shall set calipers to these five images and decribe how these illustrations influenced Beethoven in his "Orpheus" Concerto.

**Fig. 7.** Title page of Biehl-Naumann, *Orpheus und Euridice* (Kiel, 1878), the score in Beethoven's library. Courtesy of the Music Divison of the Österreichische Nationalbibliothek, Vienna.

### DOROTHEA BIEHL'S TREATMENT OF THE ORPHEUS LEGEND, COPENHAGEN, 1786, WITH ITS FOCUS ON HERSILIA, THE WOMAN SCORNED

Shortly after Beethoven's death, the contents of the apartment in which he lived on the Schwarzspanier Strasse were legally inventoried. Among the works found in his library was the piano-vocal score of *Orpheus und Euridice*, an opera by Johann Gottlieb Naumann, with a libretto by Charlotte Dorothea Biehl (Fig. 7 above).[18]

---

[18] Thayer-Forbes, 1061, Appendix C, Beethoven's Estate. Regarding the composer's

This opera—the first *opera seria* ever composed to a Danish libretto and originally titled *Orpheus og Euridice*—had been premiered in Copenhagen in 1786. The score, with the vocal lines fitted with the original Danish text and a German translation, was published the following year. Because both this score and its fascinating libretto figure so significantly in our study of Beethoven's Fourth Piano Concerto, a closer examination is required.

Charlotte Biehl's libretto was partly based on an earlier *Orpheus* libretto written in Dresden in 1778 by Gottfried Ferdinand von Lindemann. Lindemann's libretto is of unusual interest because of its emphasis on the subplot of Orpheus and the Bacchantes. In operas based on this familiar legend, the theme was historically avoided since, in order to motivate the Bacchantes' murder of Orpheus, the plot would touch on the uncomfortable subject of Orpheus's misogyny.[19] Lindemann's solution to this problem had been to invent a new character, Hersilia. This woman does not figure in the narratives of Ovid or Virgil,[20] and is identified in Lindemann's list of characters as "Euridice's rival" (Euridicens Nebenbuhlerin). Hersilia is in love with Orpheus. Orpheus, however, remains true to the memory of his deceased wife, Euridice, and so he rejects Hersilia's advances. It is thus out of jealousy that Hersilia calls on her sisters, the Bacchantes, to assist her in wreaking revenge. (More about this in due course.)

When Lindemann wrote his *Orpheus* libretto, the composer originally engaged to set this text to music was Johann Gottlieb Naumann[21]—but for unknown reasons Naumann abandoned work on his score. When this *Orpheus* was eventually performed in Berlin in 1785, the composer who set Lindemann's libretto to music was Friedrich Benda. (A piano-vocal score of the Lindemann-Benda *Orpheus* was published two years later in 1787.[22])

In this same period an ambitious project was mounted at the new Court Theater in Copenhagen to produce a grand opera with a Danish libretto. (A few operettas with Danish librettos had earlier been created for this theater, but the importance of this project was that the work they envisioned would be a more serious affair.) The composer engaged for this

---

library we find the entry, "*Orpheus und Euridice* is salable." The composer of this opera is not named. By the year 1827, however, only one opera with the German title *Orpheus und Euridice* had then been published—and this is the one with which we are here concerned.

[19] See my "The Three Chapters of the Orpheus Myth as They Figure in Librettos of Operas: the Favorite Episode, the Subject Avoided, and the Theme Cultivated," in *Words on Music: Essays in Honor of Andrew Porter on the Occasion of his 75th Birthday*, edited by David Rosen and Claire Brook (Hillsdale, N.Y.: Pendragon Press, 2003), 152-170.

[20] The only Hersilia in Ovid's *Metamorphoses* is found in Book XIV. She is the wife of Romulus. In the Classical sources of the Orpheus legend there was never a "rival of Euridice."

[21] Thomas Bauman, *North German Opera in the Age of Goethe* (Cambridge: Cambridge University Press, 1985), 237n14.

[22] *Orpheus, ein Singspiel in drey Aufzügen, vom Herrn von L... zu Dresden* (Berlin: Rellstabschen Musikdruckery zu Berlin, 1787).

undertaking was Naumann, who was an active opera composer in Sweden in those years and whose work was greatly admired in Denmark as well. Doubtless it was Naumann who suggested that this first Danish *opera seria* should be based on the Orpheus legend. The librettist chosen for this opera was Charlotte Dorothea Biehl, a remarkable women who was an accomplished linguist and scholar, the author of several successful works for the Danish theater.[23] Presumably it was Naumann who also suggested that Biehl work from the *Orpheus* libretto that Lindemann had written some eight years earlier—and which Naumann knew well.

The premiere of *Orpheus og Euridice* is documented by a rare wealth of information. As we have earlier observed, this was the result of the keen interest in this work on the part of Carl Friedrich Cramer, the energetic, enterprising, and scholarly editor of his *Magazin der Musik*.

Cramer attended the rehearsals of *Orpheus og Euridice* and published his initial impressions of the work in a lengthy essay (some 2000 words long) in which he refrained from discussing the music and focused on his many reservations regarding staging and costumes.[24] A few days later he wrote a review of the actual performance, reporting his favorable impressions of the singing and acting and his admiration for Naumann's score.[25] He was particularly moved by Naumann's version of the Infernal Scene in *Orpheus og Euridice*—indicating thereby his awareness that in this scene both the librettist and the composer owed an important debt to Calzabigi and Gluck.

Cramer was particularly fascinated by the figure of Hersilia, the character whom Charlotte Biehl had borrowed from the librettist Gottfried von Lindemann. According to the review, the role was sung compellingly by a soprano named Madam Preisler, an "excellent actress" (vortrefliche Actrice). He notes that, whereas Lindemann had invented Hersilia merely as "Euridice's rival," Biehl further developed this role, now presenting Hersilia as "a Thracian princess, and the ringleader of a chorus of Bacchantes" (eine thracische Fürstin und Anführerinn eines Bacchantinnenchors). He also pointed out that in the Biehl-Naumann *Orpheus og Euridice*, Hersilia is "a most advantageous role—a role of vehemence" (a vortheilhafteste Rolle, eine Rolle der Heftigkeit). All this is of great importance to our present concern, since the spirit of the Biehl-Naumann Hersilia—this "Rolle der Heftigkeit"—would later be expressed in the finale of Beethoven's Fourth Piano Concerto—and also be anticipated in the first movement.)

---

[23] Charlotte Biehl has been the subject of several studies by modern Danish feminist writers. A brief sketch of her career is found in Inga Dahlsgard, *Women in Denmark, Yesterday and Today* (Copenhagen: Det Danske Selskab, 1980), 53-54.

[24] *Magazin der Musik*, ed. Carl Friedrich Cramer, 2 (1786): 942-50.

[25] *Ibid.*, 936-41. (These two essays were published in reversed chronological order.)

Cramer was so impressed by Biehl's libretto that he translated it into German. (Although he was German by birth, we know he was fluent in Danish. He had spent his childhood in Copenhagen, where his father was the German Chaplain to the Danish Court.) He published this translation in his *Magazin* in 1786.[26] (At a later point he published it a second time so that it could be sold separately.[27])

The libretto is preceded by a lengthy introduction that includes Cramer's German translations of the two most important Classical versions of the Orpheus legend (Virgil's *Georgics* and Ovid's *Metamorphoses*). He then discusses the problems involved in fashioning the familiar legend into an opera libretto at great length.

At the end of this discussion Cramer announces his intention to publish a piano-vocal score of this opera, and solicits subscriptions. He received about 350 subscriptions; one of the subscribers was Christian Gottlob Neefe. It is very likely that Neefe lent his copy of this score to his talented student Beethoven, who had exhibited a great enthusiasm for opera at an early age.

From the list of subscribers we also learn that only two copies were shipped to Vienna. One was purchased by the Baron de Beine, who was a zealous collector of music books and scores.[28] (This is the copy that is now owned by the Music Division of the Austrian State Library.[29]) The other copy shipped to Vienna had been ordered by Antonio Salieri. In the years 1798-1801 Beethoven studied opera composition with Salieri, and in 1799 Beethoven dedicated his Sonatas for Violin and Piano, Opus 12, to him.

It is logical to assume that the copy of the Biehl-Naumann score in Beethoven's library was the one that had been owned by Salieri. I imagine that Salieri gave this score to Beethoven when his pupil expressed an interest in using the Orpheus legend for some purpose of his own. (Beethoven would have been familiar with the circumstances surrounding the production of this piano-vocal score, going back to his years under the guidance of Neefe.)

This much is certain: Beethoven knew Charlotte Biehl's libretto, J. B. Naumann's score, and C. F. Cramer's elaborate commentary. In each of the three movements of Beethoven's Fourth Piano Concerto, there are musical events reminiscent of dramatic events encountered in the Biehl-Naumann *Orpheus und Euridice*.

---

[26]  *Ibid.*, 1085-1145 (dated December 25).
[27]  Library of Congress, Schatz 7053. This libretto is undated.
[28]  It was thanks to the Baron de Beine that Beethoven's Bonn-period cantatas on the death of Leopold II and the elevation of Leopold II survive. See Thayer-Forbes, 119.
[29]  In a communication from the Music Division of the Austrian State Library dated March 2, 2007, Dr. Andrea Harrandt reports that this score was purchased from Antiquariat Köhler in Vienna in November 1929.

### CHARLOTTE BIEHL, A WOMAN SCORNED

At this point a digression is appropriate on the subject of Dorothea Biehl, a woman scorned. To understand Charlotte Dorothea Biehl we need to dip back into the cultural scene in eighteenth-century Denmark, an era that has been called "The Age of Holberg." Although the Baron Ludwig Holberg (1684-1754) was Norwegian by birth, he became known as "the founder of Danish literature." "Perhaps no author has ever lived who had so vast an influence over his [Danish] countrymen."[30] Holberg was a satirist who delighted in exposing the absurdities and injustices of society in his day— and among the butts of his wit was the demeaning treatment of women.[31] Charlotte Biehl was one such woman. Precociously gifted, her early education was supervised by her grandfather, who taught her Greek and Latin. He also guided her to Holberg's *Peder Peers, History of Denmark,* and many comedies. As this young woman grew intellectually, her grandfather warned, "You do not wear trousers and cannot become a professor."

Nevertheless, over the years Charlotte Biehl's literary accomplishments were impressive. Among her many publications were a Danish translation of *Don Quixote,* several historical essays about the kings of Denmark, and a lengthy correspondence she had conducted with Christian VII of Denmark. In addition she wrote several plays as well as librettos for the popular music theater. Her accomplishments won her the admiration of women far and wide. To wit, when the piano-vocal score of Naumann's *Orpheus und Euridice* was advertised for subscription, 46 copies were ordered by women.

### CHARLOTTE BIEHL'S FATHER

Next we encounter the figure of Charlotte Biehl's father. He was the secretary of the Charlottenburg Academy of Fine Arts and the curator of the Royal Museum of Fine Arts. However, this man of his time became increasingly uncomfortable with his daughter's intellectual achievements. Charlotte Biehl was later to write, "Although I was almost forty-six years old when my father died, I never dared go down to the palace garden, still less to meet anyone, without having first asked his permission."

Toward the end of her life Charlotte Biehl wrote an autobiography, wittily entitled *Mit ubetydelige Levensløb* (My Insignificant Life). (It was published many years later in 1909.) Biehl's biting sarcasm can only be a reflection of her own experience as a young woman. What must have been most painful for her was the fact that, despite her talent—or perhaps even because of it—she had been kept at a distance by her own father. I suspect

---

[30] *Encyclopedia Britannica,* 14th ed., s.v. "Holberg."
[31] Most of the following information is drawn from Inga Dahlsgard, *Women in Denmark.*

that it was her father's denigration that caused Charlotte Biehl to invent, in her *Orpheus og Euridice*, the subplot character Hersilia. Hersilia is a classic example of a woman who craves the love of a man who scorns her and casts her aside. As William Congreve pointed out, "Heaven has no rage like love to hatred turned turned, nor Hell a fury like a woman scorned."

What has all this to do with Beethoven's Fourth Piano Concerto? As we shall learn in the following chapters, the basic tension in this concerto lies in the contrasting emphases of the outer movements.

The first movement, "The Song of Orpheus": Orpheus, having lost his Euridice a second time, forswears the love of women, denigrates the Bacchantes—those women who conduct orgies at the temple of his friend Bacchus—and then sings songs in praise of boys beloved by gods. The Bacchantes seek to seduce Orpheus, but he rejects them.

Third movement, "The Revenge of the Bacchantes": the Bacchantes spy Orpheus in a meadow strumming his lyre. They pounce on him, rip off his head, and toss it into the River Hebrus.

The penultimate chapter of this book—the one dealing with the third movement of the concerto—will begin with a description of Dorothea Biehl's subplot of Hersilia, the woman scorned: attempted seduction, followed by rejection leading to rage, then ultimately revenge. This sequence of emotions is present in the first and third movements of Beethoven's concerto. And, I suspect, all this owes a debt to Dorothea Biehl's Hersilia figure. (It certainly has nothing to do with Calzabigi and Gluck.)

# CHAPTER TWO

## *A Unique Musical Form Invented to Reflect a Dramatic Narrative: The* Andante con moto *of the Fourth Piano Concerto ("Orpheus in Hades")*

Our study of the musical score of Beethoven's Fourth Piano Concerto appropriately begins with its second movement, the *Andante con moto*, for two reasons: first of all, this movement has to do with the most famous episode in the Orpheus legend, the story of Orpheus's journey to Hades to rescue Euridice. With this episode both Virgil and Ovid had launched their versions of the Orpheus legend. Secondly, there are reasons to believe that the *Andante con moto* was the movement with which Beethoven began work on his Fourth Piano Concerto. In other words, the *Andante con moto* was this concerto's generative movement.

### EARLY INSIGHTS (CZERNY AND MARX)

Carl Czerny—who included the Fourth Piano Concerto among the works he had studied with Beethoven—supplies the following remarks regarding the *Andante con moto*:

> In this movement (which, like the entire concerto, belongs to the finest and most poetical of Beethoven's creations), one cannot help thinking of an antique tragic scene, and the player must feel with what intense, pathetic expression his solo is performed, in order to contrast with the powerful and austere orchestral passages, which are, as it were, gradually withdrawn. All the means of *cantabile* expression in the melody and harmony must here be called forth, and it is only during the shake [the dramatic trill that begins at measure 55 and extends through measure 61] that the power of tone rises to the highest degree, in order to die away again to the gentlest lament. It must not be played too slowly; though the pianist may restrain the time rather more than the orchestra.[1]

The characterization "an antique tragic scene" may have been Czerny's invention, but I suspect that he got this idea from Beethoven. We can only ask, then, *which* antique tragic scene?

The scene in question was identified as early as 1859 by Adolph Bernhard Marx.[2] Marx was most keenly interested in the operas of

[1] Czerny, 110.
[2] Marx, 2:87–88.

Gluck,[3] and he detected that the *Andante con moto* in question was one of several compositions in the second half of the eighteenth century and the first half of the nineteenth century that were influenced by the famous Infernal Scene in Gluck's *Orfeo ed Euridice* (Act II, Scene 1). (Romain Rolland called this "the most moving scene in all opera.") In his book on Beethoven, Marx reported a sequence of similarities between the Gluck scene and the Beethoven concerto movement. To begin, Marx pointed out that the roles of the Furies of the Underworld and the figure of Orpheus are patently represented by the musical statements of the orchestra and the solo piano. The pleading address of Gluck's Orpheus, whose voice soars higher and higher—with the text "Furies! Spectres! Disdainful shades!" (Furie! Larve! Ombre sdegnose!)—is echoed in the soaring phrases of Beethoven's piano part in mm. 28-47. The defiant cries of Gluck's chorus of Furies—"No! No! No!"—are clearly echoed by the strings in mm. 32-35 and 44-47 of Beethoven's music. Gluck's protracted *decrescendo*, representing the Furies yielding to the song of Orpheus, is similarly reflected in Beethoven's music in mm. 38-47. (See the full account of the "Musical Narrative" on pp. 42-47 below.)

FURTHER DETAILS REGARDING BEETHOVEN'S DEBT TO GLUCK

In the *Andante con moto* of the Fourth Piano Concerto, Beethoven's debt to Gluck is immediately evident in the angry opening declaration from the orchestral strings in octaves in a terse phrase five measures long—or, more accurately described, outbursts of one measure, plus two measures, plus two measures (Ex. 1).

The comparable moment in the Gluck opera is the angry declaration of the Furies as they detect the approach of Orpheus and where they, too, sing in bold octaves (Ex. 2).

In Calzabigi's text for the Infernal Scene of Gluck's *Orfeo*, the Furies of the Underworld again and again declare their thoughts in strange poetic stanzas of five lines (for which I borrow the archaic term "quintain").

> 1. Chi mai dell'Erebo
> 2. fra le caligini
> 3. sull'orme d'Ercole
> 4. e di Piritòo
> 5. conduce il piè?

(Who can this be, who from Erebus, through the murkiness, in the paths of Hercules and Pirithous, directs his footsteps?)

---

[3] In 1863 Marx published a two-volume study, *Gluck und die Oper* (Berlin: O. Janke), in which his discussion of the Infernal Scene in *Orfeo ed Euridice* may be found in 1:279ff.

Ex. 1: Beethoven, Fourth Piano Concerto, 2nd mvt., mm.1-5

Ex. 2: Gluck, *Orfeo ed Euridice* (Vienna,1762), Act II, Scene 1, mm. 24-33

(Who can this be,who from Erebus, through the murkiness, in the paths of Hercules and Pirithous, directs his footsteps?)

(These lines correspond to a tradition encountered in similar speeches from supernatural scenes in Italian operas going back more than a century before Gluck's *Orfeo*: e.g., Cavalli's *Giasone*, 1649 [Medea's speech "Dell' antro magico/stridenti cardin ..."], and Pietro Ziani's *Annibale in Capua*, 1661 ["O voi del Erebo/Numi terribili ..."].)

In Gluck's scene the Furies' outcry is ten measures long, but this projects as four measures, plus four measures, plus two measures.[4] This is what suggested to Beethoven the unusual five-measure length of the exclamation at the outset of his concerto movement (see Ex. 1 above) (i.e., with Gluck, 4+4+2; with Beethoven, 1+2+2).

In Beethoven's setting the responding statement for the piano is in classical phrases of four-plus-four. The use of such phraseology is appropriate here since the piano represents the voice of the classical song god Orpheus (Ex. 3).

Ex. 3. Beethoven, mm. 6-13

In the ensuing dialogue, as Orpheus pleads with the Furies, the phraseology between the two antagonists rapidly telescopes. This immediately brings to mind what Beethoven had done in the first movement of his "Tempest" Sonata in D Minor (only the year before), where the partners in the dialogue had been the angry voices of the storm and the pleading human spirit.[5]

---

[4] In 1806 the phraseology 4+4+2 would govern the *Larghetto* of Beethoven's Violin Concerto, and in 1826 the same phraseology would govern the *Lento assai, cantante e tranquillo* of his swansong string quartet, Opus 135.

[5] See my "Genius in the Arena of Charlatanry: The First Movement of Beethoven's 'Tempest' Sonata in Cultural Context," *Musica Franca: Essays in Honor of Frank D'Accone*, ed. Irene Alm, Alyson McLamone, and Colleen Reardon (Stuyvesant, N.Y.: Pendragon Press, 1996), 585-630, esp. 608-09.

**Table 1 "Tempest" Sonata, 1st movt., mm. 21-41**

| Storm | 2 | 2 | 1 1 1 1 1 | 1/2 | 1/2 | |
|---|---|---|---|---|---|---|
| Human spirit | 2 | 2 | 1 1 1 1 1 | 1/2 | 1/2 | (half cadence!) |

**Table 2 Fourth Piano Concerto, *Andante con moto*, mm. 1-38**

| Furies | 5 | 5 | 3 3 1 1 | 1 |
|---|---|---|---|---|
| Orpheus | 4 plus 4 | 4 plus 4 | 2 2 1 1 | then 4 |

This telescoping phraseology had earlier occurred in the Infernal Scene of the Biehl-Naumann *Orpheus und Euridice*. In the Calzibigi-Gluck Infernal Scene, the many speeches of the Furies of the Underworld and of Orpheus had existed in large separate poetic blocks. In the derivative Biehl-Naumann version, however, these speeches are gradually abbreviated and ultimately occur in brief, telescoped thrusts (Fig. 8).

When Carl Friedrich Cramer attended the dress rehearsal of *Orpheus og Euridice*, he was struck by this passage. In his report of his

**Fig. 8.** Piano-vocal score of Biehl-Naumann, *Orpheus und Euridice*, Act II, Scene 1 (the Infernal Scene), page 51. Courtesy of the Music Division of the Österreichische Nationalbibliothek, Vienna.

initial impressions of the opera, he even quoted the Furies' defiant cries in Danish: "Nei! bort, bort, herfra!"[6] This passage is strikingly similar to what Beethoven was later to do in mm. 26-47 of the second movement of his Fourth Piano Concerto.

## THE PROTRACTED *DECRESCENDO*

Marx commented that an important similarity between Beethoven's concerto movement and the Infernal Scene in Gluck's *Orfeo* was the protracted *decrescendo* representing the Furies of the Underworld yielding to the power of Orpheus's song. Beethoven could not have failed to appreciate this passage in Gluck's opera, where Calzabigi again presents the Furies' thought in a poetic quintain:

> 1. Le porte stridano
> 2. su' neri cardini
> 3. e il passo lascino
> 4. sicuro e libero
> 5. al vincitor!

("The gates screech on black hinges, and leave the path safe and free for the victor.")

Gluck's music for this thrice-repeated speech is very inventive: first, a phrase that employs an *expanding* wedge of lines between soprano and bass; then a phrase that involves a *contracting* wedge of lines between soprano and bass; and, finally, a phrase marked "calando al *pianissimo*" (Ex. 4).

In 1774 this was surely the most ingeniously prepared *decrescendo* in the history of music. Small wonder that Gluck's Infernal Scene became the most famous scene in eighteenth-century opera. Nor was the dramatic effect of Gluck's *calando al pianissimo* lost on Beethoven. (See his version in mm. 35-47 of the "Musical Narrative" below, pp. 42-47 below.)

## FRIEDRICH AUGUST KANNE'S *ORPHEUS, EINE GROSSE OPER IN ZWEY AUFZÜGEN* (VIENNA, 1807)

Another Orpheus opera that has a bearing on this work premiered in Vienna at the Court Theater in November 1807 (only eight months after the first performance of the concerto): *Orpheus, eine große Oper in zwey Aufzügen* (Orpheus, a Large Opera in Two Acts). Both the libretto and score of this opera were the work of the same man, Friedrich August Kanne (1778-1833). Kanne was something of a phenomenon. Educated in philosophy and theology, he was an exceedingly learned man. Besides being a linguist, historian, aesthetician, and journalist, he was also a fairly prolific and fairly successful composer.[7]

---

[6] *Magazin der Musik* 2 (1786): 945.
[7] A useful study of Kanne is Hermann Ulrich, "Beethoven's Freund Friedrich August Kanne," *Österreichische Muzikzeitung* 29 (1974): 75-80.

Ex. 4. Gluck, *Orfeo*, end of Act II, Scene 1

a. mm. 255-64

b. mm. 271-80

c. mm. 281-92

Kanne and Beethoven became close friends over the years. (Kanne was one of the few people whom Beethoven addressed with the familiar "du.") His best known role in the world of scholarship was as a journalist-champion of Beethoven's music, especially during the 1820s.[8] Warren Kirkendale has advanced the convincing suggestion that Kanne was the "learned specialist" who assisted Beethoven in the many theological problems he had with the composition of the *Missa solemnis*.[9] Kanne himself composed a *Missa solemnis*, and also wrote a history of the Mass that has not survived. (He apparently destroyed his manuscript when the Jesuit censors forbade its publication. In that way Kanne protected himself from their notorious wrath.)

How early in their acquaintance Kanne and Beethoven became good friends and how soon they might have developed a vital exchange

[8] Imogen Fellinger, "Friedrich August Kanne als Kritiker Beethovens," in *Bericht über den internationalen musikwißenschaftlichen Kongreß Bonn 1970*, edited by Carl Dahlhaus et al. (Kassel: Bärenreiter Verlag, 1972), 383-86.

[9] Warren Kirkendale, "New Roads to Old Ideas in Beethoven's *Missa solemnis*," *The Musical Quarterly* 56 (1970): 665-701, esp. 700-01.

of ideas, we do not know. They had been introduced to one another by late in the year 1804, as is reported in a letter, dated December 29, from Georg August Griesinger to Breitkopf und Härtel, for whom he served as an agent:

> Kanne from Delitzsch is now here. I have led him to Haydn, Beethoven, and others. He appears to have no small opinion of his own talent, nor does he doubt that he will have success here with that talent. Given the competition among the truly great masters here, however, that will not be so easy. Haydn, Mozart, Vogler, Beethoven, Salieri are all native here. One must not just equal them to gain recognition, one must surpass them.[10]

What Beethoven and Kanne both enjoyed during these middle years of the decade was the friendship and patronage of Franz Josef Lobkowitz, in whose palace Kanne was frequently a guest.[11] In 1807 Prince Lobkowitz became a vice-director of the Royal Imperial Court Theater; it was doubtless though his influence that Kanne obtained the commission to compose his *Orpheus* for that theater.[12] At that same time it was in the *Eroica-Saal* of the Palais Lobkowitz that Beethoven's Fourth Piano Concerto was first performed.

As far as the relationship between Kanne's *Orpheus* and the *Andante con moto* of Beethoven's Fourth Piano Concerto is concerned, the arresting link occurs at the end of the first act of Kanne's opera. In the Calzabigi-Gluck *Orfeo*—which is in three acts—the famous Infernal Scene had been positioned as Act II, Scene 1. Kanne's version of the story—as he states on his title page—is restructured in two acts. This new arrangement allowed him to position the Infernal Scene to serve as a fast-moving finale of Kanne's Act I.

That finale involves a burst of spectacle. The Furies thrust their torches toward Orpheus—but he, protected by the music of his lyre, strides fearlessly through the wall of fire and arrives at the portal to Hades in triumph.

In the text of this Act I finale, one detects the ghost of Calzabigi. In general Kanne has taken the expansive and artificial speeches of the Italian poet, put them on high heat, and reduced them to their very essence. For example, when Calzabigi's Furies spy the approach of Orpheus, they exclaim in lofty language:

---

[10] Wilhelm Hitzig, "Aus dem Briefen Griesingers an Breitkopf & Härtel entnommene Notizen über Beethoven," *Der Bär* 4 (1927): 31.

[11] Ullrich, "Beethoven's Freund Friedrich August Kanne," 75.

[12] In 1807 Beethoven applied to this same company of vice-directors for an appointment to compose operas on a regular basis. He took this move at the suggestion of Lobkowitz (Thayer-Forbes, 425-27).

> 1. Chi mai dell'Erebo
> 2. fra le caligini
> 3. sull'orme d'Ercole
> 4. e di Piritòo
> 5. conduce il piè?

Kanne takes these five lines, strips them of all classical allusions and reduces them down to a single line of seven monosyllables:

> Ha! Wer wagt es hier zu nah'n?
> (Hah! Who dares approach this place?)

As a result of this incisive approach the entire text of the Act I finale of Kanne's *Orpheus* fits onto a single page of the printed libretto (Fig. 9).

*One is struck by the fact that the one-line speeches on this page (the opening lines, in particular) can be placed under the opening phrases of the* Andante con moto *of Beethoven's concerto, and Kanne's speeches mirror the emotions expressed in Beethoven's music.* (Cf. mm. 1-38 in the "Musical Narrative" below.) The order of these lines is reversed. As Kanne reworks the scene, it is Orpheus who launches the dialogue; in Beethoven's music, it is the Furies who speak first. (Beethoven, of course, was working on the familiar model of Calzabigi and Gluck.)

This relationship can only have come about as a result of communication between Beethoven and Kanne. Is it possible that Beethoven worked from Kanne? Hardly! The only logical explanation is that in late 1804 when the friendship between the two men was developing, Beethoven performed this composition for Kanne, explaining in detail how the story of Orpheus in Hades had inspired this piece.[13]

### INTERMEDIO: THE PARALLEL CASE OF KARL AMENDA AND THE *ADAGIO AFFETTUOSO ED APPASSIONATO* OF BEETHOVEN'S STRING QUARTET IN F MAJOR, OP. 18, NO. 1

Back in the summer of 1799 Beethoven had had a similar experience with his cherished friend Karl Amenda. Before Amenda left Vienna (whereafter he and Beethoven never saw one another again), the composer performed for him the *Adagio affettuoso ed appassionata* movement of his String Quartet in F Major, op. 18, no. 1.

He asked Amenda what he imagined this music to be expressing. Amenda replied, "It pictured for me the parting of two lovers." "Good!" answered Beethoven, "I thought of the scene in the burial vault in Romeo and Juliet."[14]

---

[13] See my "Orpheus Revisited: A Ten-Year Retrospect on the *Andante con moto* of Beethoven's Fourth Piano Concerto," *19th-Century Music* 19, no. 1 (1995), 33-49, especially 36-37.

[14] Thayer-Forbes, 261. For a transcription of Beethoven's sketches with his explicit descriptions of the musical symbols below the notes, see Myron Schwager, "Beethoven's Programs: What is Provable?" *The Beethoven Newsletter* 4 (1989): 49-55.

18         Orpheus.

(Unter dem stärksten Donner stürzen die Felsen ein, und
man st·ht den Eingang in die Unterwelt, aus dem mehr
rere Larven mit Flambeaus hervortreten.)

## Dreyzehnte Scene.

Orpheus und Chor der Geister.

Finale.

Orpheus.

Ich wandle froh die Schreckensbahn
Chor.
Ha! wer wagt es hier zu nah'n!
Orpheus.
Ich suche meines Lebens Glück.
Chor.
Ha! Verwegner geh zurück.
Orpheus.
Ihr Saiten rauscht im hellen Chor.
Chor.
Du betäubst nicht unser Ohr.
Orpheus.
Eröffnet mir das dunkle Thor.
Chor.
Nimmer öffnet sich dieß Thor.
Du dringst mit keiner Macht
In Orkus finstre Nacht.
Orpheus.
Ich bebe nicht vor Orkus Nacht,
Mich schützt der Töne Zaubermacht.
Chor.
Zurück! Zurück! Zurück!
Du kennst nicht Plutos Macht.

**Fig. 9**. Libretto of Kanne's *Orpheus* (Vienna, 1807), Act I finale, page 18. Courtesy of
the Music Division, Österreichische Nationalbibliothek, Vienna.

Not only was this intensely emotional piece of music inspired by that famous scene in Shakespeare's play, it was also influenced by events that occur in three widely-performed *Romeo and Juliet* operas from the end of the eighteenth century, all of which were known to Beethoven.

- *Romeo und Julie*, a *Singspiel* by Georg Benda. This was performed in Bonn in 1782 when the eleven-year-old Beethoven was already organist in the court chapel and harpsichordist in the court theater.
- *Romeo et Juliette*, by Daniel Steibelt with a French libretto. This opera was premiered in Paris in 1793. That same year the full score was published—and it can be demonstrated that Beethoven had access to this score and was strongly influenced by it. (In Beethoven's sketches for this movement, a dozen musical thoughts are fitted with captions in French derived from the scene in the crypt in Steibelt's libretto.)
- *Giuletta e Romeo*, by Antonio Zingarelli. This opera was successfully performed in Vienna in 1797 and even more successfully revived in 1804. The role of Romeo was sung by Girolomo Crescentini, the most famous castrato of his time. Crescentini actually composed the music for Romeo and recorded all of his ornamentations. His hallmark virtuosity—unusually long, soaring phrases—clearly influenced Beethoven's *Adagio affettuoso ed appassionato*.

In sum, when Beethoven set out to compose an instrumental work based on a famous story in history, he did his homework. He studied the historical texts and explored the treatments by the opera composers of his own time.[15]

Beethoven's *Adagio affettuoso ed appassionato* of his first string quartet served as a forerunner of the *Andante con moto* of his Fourth Piano Concerto. There would, however, be a very important difference between these two undertakings. In the string quartet the story of Romeo and Juliet affects only the second movement. In the concerto the story of Orpheus drives the entire work from the first phrase of first movement to the last page of the finale.

Returning to Beethoven performing the *Andante con moto* of what would become the Fourth Piano Concerto for his new friend Kanne, the latter was fascinated by Beethoven's explanation of this terse dramatic piece of music ... so fascinated that he later drew on Beethoven's musical dialogue for the first act finale in the libretto of his *Orpheus*.[16]

---

[15] For more information about this subject see my "Orpheus Revisited," 32-33.

[16] The manuscript score of Kanne's *Orpheus* is found in the Music Division of the Österreichische Nationalbibliothek in Vienna. It contains no musical similarities to Beethoven's concerto.

THE GESELLSCHAFT EDITION'S ILLUSTRATION OF ORPHEUS IN HADES AND ITS
REFLECTIONS IN KANNE AND BEETHOVEN

In Kanne's two-act *Orpheus* the finale of the second act is also of interest
and, for the purposes of this present Beethoven study, equally relevant.
This finale deals with the famous moment in the Orpheus story when
the hero breaks his vow, turns around to look at Euridice, and loses her a
second time. Kanne fills this scene with great theatrical suspense by means
of the elaborate expansion of a single line that appears in Virgil's account
of the legend:

> In that moment all his toil was spent. The ruthless tyrant's pact was broken.
> And three times a crashing noise was heard in the swamps of Avernis.
> (Terque fragor stagnis auditus Avernis.)

The imagery of the three crashes (three strokes of lightning and thunder)
is so vivid that even when artists depicting this scene were basing their
interpretation on the narrative of Ovid, they would borrow these three
dramatic crashes from Virgil's account. The example that Beethoven would
have known is found in the illustration of this scene that appeared in the
Gesellschaft edition of Ovid's *Metamorphoses of 1791* (see Fig. 10). Although
this illustration is intended to depict Ovid's version of the Orpheus story,
there are three unnatural but dramatic shafts of light in the sky: clearly the
artist's borrowing of Virgil's "Terque fragor stagnis auditus Avernis."[17]

    The setting for the Act II finale of Kanne's *Orpheus* is "a forest region
with the rocky portal to Hades in the background." Three characters (plus
a chorus) are on stage: Abrastos, the father of Euridice; Echion, the High
Priest of Apollo; and Chares, a friend of Orpheus. They are discussing their
concern for Orpheus and Euridice. The first rumble of thunder is heard.
Echion says:

> Hold on! A battle of the elements
> suddenly arises. Threatening storms
> inform me that the dark mystery
> will soon be resolved before our eyes.

The thunder then increases ("Der Donner wird stärker"). The chorus
exclaims:

---

[17] Mention of Virgil's lightning-and-thunder detail also appears in the program of Dittersdorf's *Orphée et Euridice* symphony, which had been performed in Vienna in 1786.
Dittersdorf's program was published by J. T. Hermès that same year, and is reprinted in
Carl Krebs, *Dittersdorfiana* (Berlin: Gebrüder Paetel, 1900), 177-79. Dittersdorf's score is lost,
but his program was based on Ovid. Nonetheless, at this moment when Orpheus breaks
his vow, Hermès says: "One is reminded that despite the 'protinus illa relapsa est' [and instantly she fell back into the darkness], it is not the lightning that kills Euridice." Obviously
Dittersdorf's programatic symphony had included musical depictions of lightning.

*Eurÿdice wird dem Orpheus wieder entrißen*

**Fig. 10.** *"Euridice est ravie à Orphée, pour n'avoir pas pu rèsister au plaisir de la regarder avant d'être sorti du sèjours des ombres"* (caption in the Paris edition, Vol. III, 1769.) Painter Jean-Michel Moreau "le jeune," engraving by François Denis Née. *"Eurÿdice wird dem Orpheus entris-sen"* (caption in the Viennese Gesellschaft edition, 1791.) Engraving by Joseph Stöber. Courtesy of the Department of Printing and Graphic Arts, Houghton Library, Harvard College Library.

> Hah! The wrath of the elements
> threatens mightily ...
> O Zeus, protect us in your mercy!

Whereupon the lightning and thunder break forth with tremendous violence. At this moment Orpheus and Euridice appear at the entrance of the cavern of Hades. Euridice cries out "We are saved!" Orpheus—a moment too soon—turns around to look at Euridice ... and instantly she vanishes. ("Orpheus sieht sich nach ihr um; in diesem Augenblick verschwindet sie.") One suspects that Kanne was inspired in this elaborate theatrical invention by the imagery found in the Gesellschaft edition—an illustration that was known to at least four hundred Ovid enthusiasts in Vienna at that time.

In the last decades of the eighteenth century, the world of theater experienced a rampant vogue for the depiction of storm scenes. This vogue had been made possible by modern technology. Exciting flashes of reflected light from newly-invented mantle lamps and newly-invented reflective lenses could now depict lightning, and blasts of noise from newly-invented sheets of rolled iron could now replicate thunder.

Kanne structures these events into his libretto by expanding the drama in three progressive stages—all of this inspired by Virgil's line "Terque fragor stagnis auditus Avernis."

How differently Virgil's words inspired Beethoven, who had earlier addressed the poet's imagery not by expanding it (as Kanne was to do), but by condensing the drama into nine measures of music. "Una corde, due corde, tre corde" ("one string, two strings, three strings") he instructs. Czerny comments, "Only during the shake [the dramatic trill that begins at measure 55 and extends through measure 61] does the power of tone rise to the highest degree."

Another detail in the illustration that caught Beethoven's attention is the twist of Euridice's body with her arms thrown up at an angle as she cries out to Orpheus:

> A sudden frenzy seized Orpheus, unwary in his love ... He stopped, and on the verge of light, unmindful, alas!, and vanquished in his purpose, he looked back on Euridice ... And three times a crash was heard in the swamps of Avernis. "What madness, Orpheus, what dreadful madness has ruined my unhappy self and thee?" (Virgil)
>
> And instantly she fell back (Ovid),
>
> and straightaway from his sight, like smoke mingling with thin air, she vanished afar (Virgil).

This vivid imagery inspired the string of events in the following passage in Beethoven's music (Ex. 5).

Ex. 5. mm. 55-64

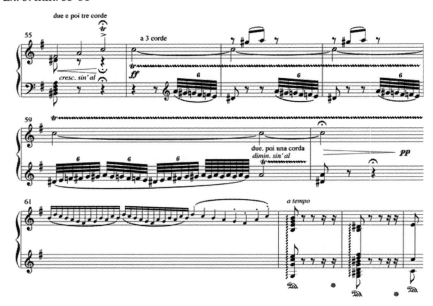

It was this passage Czerny had in mind when he wrote, "and it is only during the shake that the power of tones rises to the highest degree, in order to die away again to the gentlest lament."

### THE ROLE OF EURIDICE

In the long history of operas based on the Orpheus legend, a recurring concern for librettists was the challenge of creating a role for the character Euridice. In the accounts of the legend by both Virgil and Ovid, Euridice is all but mute. The only words that she speaks occur when Orpheus breaks his vow and Euridice cries out in despair. Opera librettists, therefore, have had to invent scenes in their Orpheus operas that would include important lines for the soprano.

The most famous example of this process is in Act III, Scene 1, of the Calzabigi-Gluck *Orfeo*, where Euridice pleads with Orpheus to turn around and give her a reassuring glance. C. F. Cramer fully appreciated the beautiful music Gluck composed for this scene, but he disapproved of the dramatic conception. In this scene, he complained, the two characters are turned into foolish children (läppische Kinder). Euridice's success in getting Orpheus to break his vow turns her into "a very ordinary woman" (eine ganz gewöhnliche Frauenzimmer), and, even worse, turns the heroic Orpheus into a hen-pecked husband. "They both deserve what they get," Cramer concluded wryly, "our sympathy is transformed into derision."

Biehl's solution was to create altogether new scenes that have nothing to do with Virgil or Ovid. One of these (Act II, Scene 3) is an elaborate monologue for Euridice (still in Hades) in which she expresses her undying devotion to her husband, from whom she has been separated. The next scene is a conversation between Euridice and Proserpina. Here Proserpina tells Euridice that Orpheus's greatest source of strength lies in *her* constancy and *her* courage. The librettist Charlotte Biehl was an important feminist in her day; in these two scenes her goal is to endow Euridice with the stature of a heroine (eine Heldin).

This particular problem of creating a role for Euridice was not a central concern for Beethoven as he composed his Fourth Piano Concerto. On the other hand, in the larger scheme of things it was essential that he communicate the story of Orpheus's second loss of his new bride and, to this end, somehow introduce the figure of Euridice. Beethoven accomplished this with utmost simplicity by going back to Virgil. In mm. 57-59 of Ex. 5, as the pianist's right hand continues that long trill, the left hand depicts the three crashes heard in the swamps of Avernis. In mm. 57 and 58, the left hand crosses above the right and plays those two brief gestures, G♯ rising to A. This can only represent Euridice's desperate cry, "Orpheus! Orpheus!" (In German, "Orpheus" is pronounced in two syllables.)

### Sulzer's Recommendation for Composers of Instrumental Music

In Germany at the end of the eighteenth century the most widely read— and widely discussed—aesthetic treatise was Johann Georg Sulzer's *Allgemeine Theorie der schönen Künste*. Among the readers of this popular treatise was the young Beethoven.[18] Sulzer concludes his lengthy article on "Instrumentalmusik" by addressing a question repeatedly raised in his day: is it possible for instrumental music—wherein no text is heard—to express human emotions?

> . . . most pieces of this sort [symphonies, concertos, sonatas, and other purely instrumental compositions] are nothing else but pleasant sound that falls upon the ear in a stormy or gentle manner. In order to avoid this [problem], the composer will do well always to imagine very distinctly the character of some person, or some situation, or some human emotion, and exercise his imagination to the point where he believes that he can hear what a person in such a situation would be saying. The composer can assist himself in this endeavor by seeking out passages in literature that are pathetic, fiery, gentle, or tender, and to declaim these passages in an appropriate voice, and then translate these emotions into his music.

The *Adagio affettuoso ed appassionato* in Beethoven's String Quartet in F Major, op. 18, no. 1, was a clear response to Sulzer's recommendation. Beethoven's Fourth Piano Concerto would do the same but on a much larger scale.

---

[18] See my "Exploring Sulzer's *Allgemeine Theorie* as a Source Used by Beethoven," *The Beethoven Newsletter* 2 (1987): 1-7.

## The musical narrative

In the following narrative a sequence of twenty-two musical events are responses to events in Kanne's libretto, Gluck's score, or the original sources of Virgil and Ovid.

### Event 1

FURIES: "Ha! Wer wagt es hier zu nahn?" (Hah! Who dares approach this place?)
Kanne, line 2; Beethoven, mm. 1-5

### Event 2[19]

ORPHEUS: "Ich wandle froh die Schreckensbahn." (I tread this path of terror gladly.)
Kanne, line 1; Beethoven, mm. 6-13

[19] Beethoven's annotation in the score: "Während des ganzen Andantes hat der Klavierspieler ununterbrochen die Verschiebung (una corda) anzuwenden, das Zeichen 'Ped.' Bezieht sich ausserdem auf den zeitweisen Gebrauch des gewöhnlichen Pedalzuges." (During the entire Andante the pianist should employ the shifting pedal [una corda] uninterruptedly; the symbol "Ped." refers to the occasional use of the customary pedal.)

### Event 3

FURIES: "Hah! Verwegner, geh zurück!" (Ha! Trespasser, go back!)
Kanne, line 4; Beethoven, mm. 14-18

### Event 4

ORPHEUS: "Ich suche meines Lebens Glück." (I seek the joy of my life.)
Kanne, line 3; Beethoven, mm. 19-25

### Events 5, 6, 7, and 8

FURIES: "Du betäubst nicht unser Ohr!" (You do not deceive us!)
Kanne, line 5; Beethoven, mm. 26-27

ORPHEUS: "Eröffnet mir das dunkle Thor."(Open to me the dark portal.)
Kanne, line 6; Beethoven, mm. 28-29

FURIES: "Nimmer öffnet sich dieß Thor!" (Never will this portal open!)
Kanne, line 7; Beethoven, mm. 30-31

### Events 9 and 10

FURIES: "Zurück! Zurück! Zurück!" (Go back! Go back! Go back!) Kanne, line 13
ORPHEUS: "Erbarmt euch! Erbarmt euch!" [from Naumann] (Have pity!
Have pity!) Beethoven, mm. 33-38

### Event 11

A nine-measure *decrescendo* expressing those lines in Gluck's opera:
"Ah, what unfamiliar sweet emotion causes our implacable fury to be
suspended?" The gates creak on their hinges and leave the passage secure
and free to the victor.
Mm. 38-46

## Event 12

Orpheus, protected by the waves of tone from his magical lyre, leads Euridice through the gloom of the Underworld.
Mm. 47-51

## Event 13

But he was anxious for his wife, "out of longing and fear" (aus Sehnsucht und aus Furcht): from the 1791 Gesellschaft edition's translation of Ovid.
Mm. 52-54

## Event 14

"A suddden frenzy seized Orpheus, unwary in his love... He stopped, and on the verge of light, unmindful, alas! and vanquished in purpose, he looked back at Euridice, now his own." (Cum subita incautum dementia cepit amantum ... restitit. Euridicenque suam iam luce sub ipsa, immemor heu! victusque an imi respexit. Virgil, lines 488-91.)
Mm. 55-56

### Event 15

"In that moment all his toil was spent, the ruthless typrant's pact was broken. And three times a crash was heard in the swamps of Avernis. She cried, 'What madness, Orpheus, what dreadful madness has ruined my unhappy self and thee?'" (Ibi omnis effusus labor atque immitis rupta tyranni foedera, terque fragor stagnis auditus Avernis. Illa 'quis et me'inquit 'miseram et te perdidit, Orpheu, quis tantus furor? Virgil, lines 492-95.) Mm. 56-59

### Event 16

"And instantly she fell back." (Et protinus illa relapsa est. Ovid, line 57.) Mm. 60-61

### Event 17

"And straightaway from his sight, like smoke mingling in thin air ..."(Et ex oculis subito, ceu fumus in auras commixtus tenuis ... Virgil, lines 499-500.) M. 61

### Event 18

"... she vanished afar "( Ö fugit diversa, Virgil, line 200.) Mm. 62-64

### Event 19

"Lo, again the cruel fates call me back, and sleep veils my swimming eyes." (En iterum crudelia retro fata vocant conditque natantia lumina somnus. Virgil, lines 495-96.)
Mm. 64-69

### Event 20

"She spoke one last 'farewell,' which scarcely reached his ears." (Supremumque 'vale' quod iam vix auribus ille acciperet dixit ... Ovid, lines 62-63.)
Mm. 69-70

### Event 21

"... and she fell back to the place whence she had come" ( ... revolutaque rursus eodem est, Ovid, line 63.)
Mm. 70-72

### Event 22

"And he stretched out his arms, eager to clasp her or to feel her clasp. Unhappy one, he clasped nothing but the yielding air." (Bracchiaque intendens prendique et prendere certans nil nisi cedentes infelix arripit auras. Ovid, lines 58-59.)

These twenty-two events bring to mind Czerny's description of "a species of composition that carried instrumental music to a pitch of refinement resembling even poetry and painting. In such works we no longer hear the mere expression of feelings, we *see* fine pictures—we *hear* the narration of circumstances."[20]

## UNIQUE FEATURES OF THIS "CONCERTO" MOVEMENT

The *Andante con moto* of Beethoven's Fourth Piano Concerto is unlike any other middle movement in the history of the concerto. First of all, this movement is just seventy-two measures long; if it is performed correctly, it is the briefest second movement in the entire literature of the concerto.[21] Also, this is the only movement in any of the Beethoven piano concertos— plus the Triple Concerto—in which the solo piano abstains from its traditional supportive role as a continuo instrument.[22] Finally, as we have just observed, the form of this *Andante con moto* is unique.

The orchestration of this movement is also strange. Whereas there is a full complement of wind instruments plus two trumpets and timpani on the stage, the *Andante con moto* is scored only for strings.

The music that Beethoven wrote here for the pianist is also unusual. Nowhere is there the slightest suggestion of soloistic virtuosity. Indeed, the soloist's part in this movement can be performed by a musician with only the most limited keyboard skill. More than that, *the entire score* of this movement—orchestra alternating with solo—can likewise be performed easily by any pianist with only modest coordination. From the standpoint of its technical simplicity, this concerto movement already stands apart, in a very odd way, from every other thing of its kind in the repertory.

At no point in the progress of the movement do the soloist and the orchestra interact in the manner that music history has taught us to expect from the partners in a concerto. The string choir and the solo pianist emerge from separate worlds, but even when their differences are reconciled, they never "consort" in the manner of the soloist and the orchestra in a concerto. How does one explain this array of unconventional features in the *Andante con moto* of Beethoven's Fourth Piano Concerto?

---

[20] Czerny, 36.

[21] The second movements of Mozart's piano concertos average seven to eight minutes in performance. If the second movement of Beethoven's Fourth Piano Concerto is performed *Andante con moto*, it lasts about four minutes. Regarding the history of tempi used for this movement in recent recordings, see my "Orpheus Revisited," 29-34.

[22] See Tibor Szász, "Beethoven's *basso continuo*: Notation and Performance," *Performing Beethoven*, ed. Robin Stowell (Cambridge: Cambridge University Press, 1994), 1-22. On p. 2 Szász writes, "The only exception is the slow movement of the Piano Concerto in G Major op. 58, where keyboard continuo is excluded."

I believe that this *Andante con moto* originated as a composition for solo piano. The corollary, then, is that the subsequent concerto movement, so familiar to us all, is a transcription. The best way to test this statement is to step to the piano and perform this composition as a work for solo piano. In that way it projects as a persuasively complete experience.

THE *ANDANTE CON MOTO* OF BEETHOVEN'S FOURTH PIANO CONCERTO PERFORMED AS A PIECE FOR SOLO PIANO

In the mid-nineteenth century two great musician-composers believed that the second movement of Beethoven's Fourth Piano Concerto communicated in a compelling way when performed for solo piano. Here is a report from Fanny Mendelssohn dated May 31, 1840, who is writing to her brother about her visit to the French Academy in Rome. She tells of playing four-hand music with the director of the Academy, the painter Jean-Dominique Ingres, with the splash of a fountain in the background and with many bearded Academy students (Gounod among them) "lying about on the steps and pedestals of the pillars in a state of unmitigated astonishment ..." Following this spontaneous music making, she and Ingres "climbed up to the Campanile, where I had never been before, and from which I saw the splendid view for the last time in the light of the setting sun, not without many tears."

After dinner the piano was moved into the main hall, since the Academy's celebrated musician-guest had agreed to treat the company to an impromptu evening concert. (The instrument on which Fanny Mendelssohn performed, incidentally, had been built by the firm of Érard Frères in Paris.) "The twilight was rapidly deepening, and a peculiar sensation stole over the whole company." In this romantic setting this sensitive musician performed, among other pieces, the first movement of Beethoven's "Moonlight" Sonata. As a prelude to her salon concert, however, Fanny Mendelssohn performed the *Andante con moto* of Beethoven's Fourth Piano Concerto.[23]

Franz Liszt used this *Andante con moto* for the same purpose. His daughter, Cosima Wagner, in her diary entry for September 4, 1872, describes an intimate party hosted by Frau von Meyend (with Richard Wagner as one of the guests), at which occasion Liszt was invited to perform after dinner. As the core of his impromptu concert he played the Chopin Preludes. At Cosima's request, he then delivered his *Mephisto Waltzer* as a finale. To establish the mood for this increasingly brilliant

---

[23] Sebastian Hensel, *The Mendelssohn Family, 1729-1847*, 2 vols. (New York: Harper & Brothers, 1882), 2:119-20.

salon concert, however, Liszt chose the *Andante con moto* of Beethoven's Fourth Piano Concerto.[24]

### BEETHOVEN'S ÉRARD PIANO (PARIS, 1803)

In November 1802 Beethoven wrote an amusing letter to his friend Nikolaus Zmeskall, the subject of which was Beethoven's wish to acquire a new fortepiano of the most modern design.[25] The instrument he had in mind must have two features: first of all, it must have a mahogany veneer— mahogany being the wood of choice if one sought to have a piano with an "Empire" look. The other requirement was that the instrument must have an *una corda* pedal.

Apparently the news that Beethoven was looking for a new instrument became public knowledge for Beethoven remarks to Zmeskall, that "the whole tribe of fortepiano builders have been swarming about me in their anxiety to serve me." Indeed, less than a year later, Beethoven received the gift of a five-and-a-half-octave fortepiano of avant-garde design from the firm of Érard Frères in Paris (Fig. 11).

Yes, this instrument was finished with a mahogany veneer.[26] More important, this fortepiano was equipped with an *una corda* pedal. This new invention produced a "voice" that stood apart from the normal sound of the instrument—and was thus an invitation to dialogue. Furthermore, since the typical fortepiano of the first decade of the nineteenth century was now triple-strung from top to bottom, it could produce a clearly audible progression from *una corda* to *due corde* to *tre corde*—effects that Beethoven calls for in his *Andante con moto* with especially dramatic effect. Beethoven's uniquely detailed instructions to the pianist reveal the importance of the *una corda* pedal in the concept and the performance of this work.

> Während des ganzen Andantes hat der Klavierspieler ununterbrochen die Verschiebung [the shifting pedal] anzuwenden, das Zeichen 'Ped,' bezieht sich ausserdem auf den zeitweisen Gebrauch des gewöhnlichen Pedalzuges. (During the entire Andante the pianist should employ the shifting pedal uninterruptedly, the symbol "Ped." refers to the occasional use of the customary pedal [the damper pedal].)

[24] *Cosima Wagner's Diaries, Vol. I, 1869-1877*, ed. Martin Gregor-Dellin and Dietrich Mack, trans. Geoffrey Skelton (New York: Harcourt Brace Jovanovich, 1976), 532.
[25] Brandenburg, 1:137, letter no. 116; Anderson, 1:82-83, letter no. 66.
[26] This instrument, which is owned by the Oberösterreichisches Landesmuseum in Linz, is described in considerable detail in the *Katalogue der Sammlung alter Musikinstrumente: I. Teil, Saiteninstrumente* (Vienna: Kunsthistorisches Museum, 1966), 35-36. (For several years it had been on loan to the Kunsthistorisches Museum in Vienna so that it could be included in their carefully researched catalogue.)

Fig. 11. Beethoven's Érard fortepiano (Paris, 1803). Courtesy of the Oberöster-richisches Landesmuseum, Linz.

I believe that the second movement of the Fourth Piano Concerto came into being as Beethoven experimented with the dramatically expressive possibilities of his new Érard fortepiano.

## INFORMATION IN THE SKETCHES

As regards the chronology of Beethoven's work on this *Andante con moto* we have two precious bits of information recently published by Martha Frohlich.[27] On a single sheet of sketches in Beethoven's hand known as the Friskin Bifolium are found ideas about the opening dialogue between the orchestral strings and the solo piano. On the basis of watermark studies by Alan Tyson, the Friskin Bifolium can be dated "around 1806"—that is from the period when Beethoven was laboring on the completion of this concerto.

Frohlich then reports a brief but teasing note about the second movement of this concerto that Beethoven jotted on an isolated page from another dismembered sketchbook known as Autograph 19e, Fascicle C (SV 29). (This is found in the Staatsbibliothek in Berlin.)

> 2da parte solament[e] / fin al trillo / mit vielen 16 tel / triolen / bis zum Triller auf der cadenz nach E mo[ll] (second part only until the trill, with many 16th-note triplets until the trills on the cadence to E minor)

This fragmentary page, Tyson explains, was written "not before ca. May or June 1804."

What is the composer saying to himself in this teasing fragment when he writes, "until the trill [singular], with many 16th-note triplets until the trills [plural] on the cadence to E minor"? These words can only refer to that intensely dramatic passage in mm. 55-61, which begins with a trill (singular) that expands into a sequence of trills (plural). *These measures, as we now know, have to do with that crucial moment when Orpheus breaks his vow.* And so, perhaps as early as May or June of 1804, we find Beethoven recording ideas having to with the Infernal Scene from the Orpheus legend. At what point, we may wonder, did Beethoven arrive at the vision of an entire concerto based on that legend?

One thing we do know is that, in the last months of 1804 Beethoven met his fascinating new friend, Kanne.

## THE CONCEPT OF THE GENERATIVE MOVEMENT

In the vast literature about Beethoven, scholars have rarely asked which movement in a multi-movement work was composed first. In most cases the question is unanswerable and in many cases unimportant.

One recalls, however, Czerny's remark that "in many of his finest compositions Beethoven was inspired by visions drawn either from his reading, or created by his own excited imagination." In cases of this sort we may enquire which of the several movements—of a sonata, string quartet, symphony, or concerto—was the first to be thus inspired? In the answer to that question comes the revelation of the "generative" movement.

---

[27] Martha Frohlich, "Sketches for Beethoven's Fourth and Fifth: a Long-Neglected Source," *Bonner Beethoven-Studien* 1 (1999): 29-48.

With the "Kreutzer" Sonata it is clear that the finale was composed in 1802; the first and second movements were composed the following year to serve as experiences that would drive toward that finale. In other words, the finale of the "Kreutzer" Sonata was the source of inspiration for the first two movements.[28] Similarly, Lewis Lockwood's thoughtful studies of the sketches of the *Eroica* Symphony make it clear that the generative movement of that work was again its finale. (The *Eroica* Symphony was composed a year after the "Kreutzer" Sonata.) Lockwood's chapter "The Earliest Sketches for the *Eroica* Symphony" concludes with his revelation that "In the end was the beginning."[29] In contrast to these two clear cases (the "Kreutzer" Sonata and the *Eroica* Symphony—both of which were generated by their final movements), Beethoven's Fourth Piano Concerto was generated by its central movement. In this case the generative force derived from the most gripping moment in the Orpheus legend; this force would then inspire the concerto's first and third movements.

---

[28] See my "The Kreutzer Sonata as Dialogue," esp. 36.

[29] Lewis Lockwood, *Beethoven: Studies in the Creative Process* (Cambridge, Mass.: Harvard University Press, 1992), 150.

# CHAPTER THREE

## The Orpheus Legend as a Unifying Force:
## The First Movement of the Fourth Piano Concerto
## ("The Song of Orpheus")

### CYCLIC ORGANIZATION

Beethoven's interest in cyclic organization came to a peak in a group of important works dating from the years 1804-1808. In these compositions we observe that not only are all the movements in a single opus unified by an extramusical idea, but throughout the entire work there is a meaningful stream of thought with a concomitant flow of emotions expressed in the music—all based on that idea.

The best example is the *Pastoral* Symphony. The Symphony in C Minor is a similarly unified composition. All four of its movements employ that famous short-short-short-long motive. But the plot of the Symphony in C Minor is very different.

Both these works were premiered at Vienna's Theater-an-der-Wien on December 22, 1808. That amazing concert began with the *Pastoral* Symphony, which was announced as Beethoven's "Fifth" Symphony. After the intermission, the Symphony in C Minor was performed, and this was announced as his "Sixth." (The later switch in the numbering reflected the order in which these works were published. Beethoven's original numbering is of extreme significance since these two symphonies are pendants, the *Pastoral* Symphony preparing the ground for its sequel, the Symphony in C Minor.)[1]

At the concert of December 22, 1808, the first public performance of Beethoven's Fourth Piano Concerto took place between the *Pastoral* Symphony and the Symphony in C Minor. This concerto is also a cyclic work, its three movements based on the three standard "chapters" of the Orpheus legend: "The Song of Orpheus" (the first movement); "Orpheus in Hades" (the second movement); and "Orpheus and the Bacchantes" (the finale).[2]

[1] See my "Beethoven's Philosophical Monologue Regarding the Route to Rescue from His Fate: The *Andante con moto* of His Symphony in C Minor," *The Beethoven Journal* 22 (2007): 50-86.

[2] The history of these three recurring chapters is discussed in considerable detail in my article "The Three Chapters of the Orpheus Myth As They Figure in Librettos of Operas: the favorite Episode, the Subject Avoided, and the Theme Cultivated."

## CZERNY'S HINTS REGARDING THE FOURTH PIANO CONCERTO AS A CYCLIC WORK

Czerny's characterization of the *Andante con moto* of the Fourth Piano Concerto as "an antique tragic scene" was made in the following context:

> In this movement, (which, like the entire *concerto* [Czerny's italics], belongs to the finest and most poetical of Beethoven's creations), one cannot help thinking of an antique tragic scene ...[3]

The original German version of the phrase in parentheses is "der, wie überhaupt das ganze *Concert*, zu Beethovens schönsten und poesiereichsten Schöpfungen gehört." With this comment, "like the entire *concerto*," Czerny reveals an awareness that the poetic idea that plays such an important role in the second movement of the Fourth Piano Concerto is at work in the other two movements as well. On the next page of his treatise Czerny states that

> the finale of this concerto stands in a certain connection with the foregoing, in order to complete the picturesque design ...
>
> (steht in einem gewißen Zusammenhang mit dem hervorgehenden, um das pittoreske Gemälde zu ergänzen ...)

This observation further suggests that Czerny was aware of the existence of a specific unifying poetic plan in the Fourth Piano Concerto. As we shall observe in the pages ahead, an amazing array of similarities between details in Ovid's text and details in Beethoven's music support the conclusion that all three movements of the Fourth Piano Concerto were inspired by the Orpheus legend.

## BEETHOVEN'S MODUS OPERANDI—AND OUR MODUS OPERANDI

In the second movement of this concerto, Beethoven's approach to the Classical accounts of the Orpheus legend was to compose an event-by-event musical narrative. In order to achieve his goal, he had to create a unique musical form. In the first and third movements—"The Song of Orpheus" and "Orpheus and the Bacchantes"—Beethoven worked very differently. In these two chapters of Ovid's text one rarely encounters passages that invite, or even permit, narrative treatment in music. More importantly, the elaborate conventions of the musical forms associated with the first and third movements of classical concertos forbade such an approach—*and Beethoven did not abandon these forms.* The composer's ingenuity thus led him in other directions.

In his framing movements Beethoven worked along four lines:

1. In the opening pages of each movement a sequence of musical ideas closely reflects a sequence of thoughts that occur at the outset of these two episodes in the narrative of Ovid.

---

[3] Czerny, 110.

2. As Beethoven's musical forms progress, important subordinate themes are fashioned to reflect important subsequent events in Ovid's stories.

3. As the logical next step, the development sections of these two musical forms are based on the central conflicts in the stories found in these two chapters of Ovid's version of the Orpheus legend.

4. Finally, the last pages of these two movements bring each chapter to an appropriate conclusion. To wit, at the end of the first movement Beethoven lingers on the three most important concerns in "The Song of Orpheus" (more on this in due course). At the end of the finale Beethoven creates an elaborate string of events that provide a dénouement not only for that movement but for the whole adventure with the Orpheus legend.

Of all Beethoven's music, the Fourth Piano Concerto is his most intensely poetic invention.[4] As we continue to explore this exquisite work, we would do well to first consider the steps the composer took as he approached the creation of his "Orpheus" Concerto. His first challenge was to arrive at a close familiarity with his sources—literary, pictorial, and operatic. Informed and inspired as he was by these sources, he was finally prepared to compose a concerto that would involve a constant flow of musical details expressive of the story. Again and again in this adventure he arrived at musical details that involved fascinating departures from the norms of the Classical piano concerto.

Our first challenge is to identify and analyze the musical details that embody those fascinating departures from the norms of the Classical piano concerto. Informed by our technical analysis of the music, we then ask, why these departures? (The answers to those questions are what Chapters 2-4 are all about.)

What is involved here is simply role reversal. The composer studies his sources and arrives at unique artistic inventions. The historian studies the composer's unique artistic inventions and arrives at explanations found in the composer's sources. In the introductory moment of Beethoven's "Orpheus" Concerto we find the quintessential example of this process.

THE INTRODUCTION: ORPHEUS TESTS THE STRINGS OF HIS LYRE—AND ALL NATURE RESPONDS IN AMAZEMENT (THE DEPICTION IN THE GESELLSCHAFT EDITION)

The first movement begins not with the usual orchestral tutti but with a very quiet phrase by the solo piano. This phrase, we note, is five measures long. (A unifying device in Beethoven's Fourth Piano Concerto is that all three movements begin with musical thoughts that involve five, or at most

---

[4] The reader will immediately think of many other Beethoven works that deserve to be called "poetic." Beethoven's Fourth Piano Concerto stands apart from those, however, since it is so densely and consistently inspired by poetic imagery that can be precisely identified.

ten, measures. This process originated in the second movement and goes back to those poetic quintains in Calzabigi's libretto.) The first chord in this phrase employs eight notes—and when Czerny quotes this phrase he indicated that these eight notes should be gently arpeggiated (Ex. 7).

Ex. 7. 1st movt., mm. 1-5. Facsimile from Czerny, p. 109

Ovid says that before Orpheus begins his song, with which he will enchant all of nature, he

> tested the many strings of his lyre by strumming them with his thumb [i.e., not with the ivory plectrum with which the Greek lyre was normally played]; and though these were of many different pitches, they were in harmony with one another.

> (Ut satis impulsas temptavit pollice chordas et sensit varios, quamvis diversa sonarent, concordare modos ... Book X, lines 145-47).

This five-measure phrase is left hanging on the dominant.

According to Ovid, as Orpheus prepares to sing his song, he is seated in an open meadow "devoid of shade"; but, in response to the very sound of his magical lyre, "shade came to that place." (Collis erat collemque super planissima campi area, quam viridem faciebant graminis herbae: umbra loco deerat; qua postquam parte resedit dis genitus vates et fila sonantia movit, umbra loco venit. Book X, lines 86-90.) With characteristic fervor Ovid describes nature's response to the sound of the lyre by naming no fewer than twenty-seven species of trees, bushes, and vines that uproot themselves and assemble around Orpheus to provide a protective bower for the musician.

The illustration of this scene in the Gesellschaft edition of the *Metamorphoses* (1791) depicts Orpheus seated in a shady grove, surrounded by a crowd of exotic animals who have been drawn by the sound of the musician's lyre (Fig. 12).

In contrast to Ovid's effusive naming of twenty-seven species of flora, Beethoven works succinctly. In response to the solo piano's opening phrase, the strings (minus the basses) enter **pp**. This entrance is in the key of B Major. Coming from the D-major chord (the dominant of G), B Major creates a weird cross relationship. The quiet D in the bass at measure 5,

**Fig. 12.** "*Orphée sur le mont Rhodope attire au son de sa voix et de sa lyre les animaux, les roches, at les arbres*" (caption in the Parisian edition, Vol. III, 1769.) Painter Charles Eisen, engraving by N. De Launay. "*Orpheus zieht durch sein Saitenspiel Thiere, Felsen, und Bäume an sich*" (caption in the Viennese Gesellschaft edition, 1791). Engraving by Kilian Ponheimer. Courtesy of the Department of Printing and Graphic Arts, Houghton Library, Harvard College Library.

is, in the next measure, lifted to a *very* quiet D♯ in the second violin. The resulting sense of hushed surprise is probably Beethoven's response to Ovid's line describing the magic of the moment: "and shade came to that place" (Ex. 8).

Ex. 8. Mm. 6-14

### The Orchestral Tutti: Orpheus's *Proemium*

In the aftermath of these two introductory events, the conventional orchestral tutti begins with the return to the home key at measure 14. (Beethoven "punctuates" the moment by having the basses enter pizzicato.) At this point Beethoven launches a sequence of musical ideas systematically reflective of details encountered in lines 148-154, Book X, of Ovid's text. As teachers of Greek and Latin are fond of pointing out, these seven lines constitute the definitive example of a Classical *proemium*.

A Classical *proemium* opens with the poet's declaration of his main goal as an artist, and then proceeds with an explanation of his specific intent in the poem to follow. The *proemium* Ovid invents for Orpheus delivers six thoughts:

[1] O Muse, my mother, let Jove inspire my song. [2] Oft' have I sung the power of Jove before. All things yield to the power of Jove! [3] In a heavy strain I have sung about giants, and victorious shafts hurled in all directions on the Phlegraean plains. [4] Now, however, I have no need

for the gentler touch, [5] for I would sing of boys beloved by gods; [6] and about maidens who are inflamed by unnatural love and pay the penalty for their lust.

148   ab Iove, Musa parens, (cedunt Iovis omnia regno),
149   carmina nostra move! Iovis est mihi saepe potestas
150   dicta prius:⁵ cecini plectro graviore Gigantes
151   sparsaque Phlegraeis victricia fulmina campis.
152   nunc opus est leviore lyra, puerosque canamus
153   dilectos superis, inconcessisque puellas
154   ignibus attonitas meruisse libidine poenam.

At measure 14 the orchestra picks up on the rhythmic motive up-up-up-down, which the solo piano had introduced in measures 1-2, and which occurs again in measures 6-7 in the response of the strings. As is well known, Beethoven had used this terse motive on a couple of earlier occasions,⁶ but for very different purposes. In this new case, the recurring, almost obsessive use of this motive seems to relate to Orpheus's wish that his music should constantly be inspired by Jove: "O Muse, my mother, let Jove inspire my song"; "Oft' have I sung the power of Jove before." I assume that, in the first movement of the Fourth Piano Concerto, Beethoven's ubiquitous short-short-short-long motive functions as a symbol for the omnipresent influence of Jove (Ex. 9).

These measures then lead to a brief but urgent *crescendo*, which at the end builds to music that seems to express a sense of determination. Says Orpheus, "All things yield to the power of Jove!" (Ex. 10, see p. 62).

At measure 29 the tonality shifts to A Minor, and the mood changes abruptly (Ex. 11, see p. 63).

## INTERMEZZO: THE *GRAVIORE LYRA* VS. THE *LEVIORE LYRA*

To understand what inspired Beethoven as he composed these measures— and those that follow—a brief digression will be helpful. Greek poets regularly separated their writings into two categories: poems that had to do with battles, warriors, and heroes—and, in contrast, poems that had to do with love. To make this distinction, these poets were fond of a

---

⁵ The astute reader will observe that in my translation of these first two lines I have located Orpheus's exclamation "cedunt Iovis omnia regno!" at the end of "thought 2" ("All things yield to the power of Jove"). This revised sequence reflects the emotional *crescendo* in measures 14-29 of Beethoven's music.

⁶ In the first movement of the Piano Sonata in E♭ Major, op. 31, no. 3, and in the first movement of the Piano Sonata in F Minor, op. 57. Soon after Beethoven completed his Fourth Piano Concerto he composed his Symphony in C Minor—and that symphony, of course, uses the short-short-short-long motive in all four movements as the bearer of the symphony's message about victory over fate. See my "'Let Your Deafness No Longer be a Secret—Even in Art': Self-Portraiture and the Third Movement of the C Minor Symphony," *Beethoven Forum* 8 (2000): 25-70.

Ex. 9. Mm. 14-18

Ex.10. Mm. 18-29

Ex. 11. Mm. 29-32

having to do with the lyre itself. Poems about battles and heroes employed the *graviore lyra* (the "serious lyre") while poems about love employed the *leviore lyra* (the "gentle lyre").

This distinction was known in Beethoven's world, as is revealed in Schubert's song "An die Leier" (Schubert Complete Edition, no. 414; New Edition, no. 737), which was composed in 1822 or 1823. The text of this song was by F. S. Ritter von Bruchmann; it is a free translation of a poem by the first century b.c.e. Greek poet Anacreon, whose name is virtually synonymous with love poetry, as in the expression "Anacreontic verse." In Schubert's "An die Leier" the poet sings songs in praise of heroic warriors but his lyre, even after repeated efforts, refuses to cooperate. Anacreon's lyre will respond only to songs of love.

> So lebt denn wohl, Heroen,
> denn meine Saiten tönen,
> statt Heldensang zu drohen,
> nur Liebe im Erklingen.

(Farewell then, you heroes; for instead of threatening with heroic songs, my strings perform only in order to ring forth [with songs] about love.)

This conventional contrast between the *graviore lyra* and the *leviore lyra* figures importantly in lines 150-52 of the *proemium* of Ovid's "Song of Orpheus"—and it figures importantly in Beethoven's music, as well.

In Ex. 11 Beethoven instructs the cellos and basses to play pizzicato. As far as I know, this is the first occasion in the opening tutti of any Classical concerto where the basses are asked to perform pizzicato. When Orpheus remarks that he formerly sang songs about warriors and battles (in the spirit of the *graviore lyra*), he did so by playing his lyre with a "plectro graviore." Presumably it was the words "plectro graviore" that—in this passage, in this area of the Classical form—suggested to Beethoven the innovative use of pizzicato in the basses.

In this same example the line for the basses repeatedly uses ascending intervals that leap over a range of more than an octave. These would have been suggested by Ovid's vivid image about "victorious shafts hurled in all directions on the Phlegraean plains."

What is most striking in mm. 27-40, however, is the tonal adventure. Tovey comments about this passage, where "the tonality modulates through a considerable range of keys" (Ex. 12).[7] Here are the specifics of this modulation through a considerable range of keys:

| | | | |
|---|---|---|---|
| 27 | G Major | 33 | (very abruptly) C Major |
| 28 | G Major to A Minor | 34-36 | C Major to B Minor |
| 29 | A Minor | 37 | (very abruptly) G Major |
| 30-32 | A Minor to E Minor | 48-50 | G Major to F♯ Minor |

---

[7] Tovey, 76.

Ex. 12. Mm. 33-40

In sum, in a passage just fourteen measures long Beethoven touches on six keys—winding up in F♯ Minor!

In the opening tutti of the first movement of a typical Mozart concerto, it is not at all unusual to find a very brief venture away from the home key. To touch upon *five* other keys in quick succession in the opening pages of the first movement of a Classical concerto is, however, unprecedented. Better said, audacious! What can have suggested this bizarre tonal excursion?

Once more, the answer is found in the line "[and I sang of] victorious shafts hurled in all directions on the Phlegraean plains" (sparsaque Phlegraeis victricia fulmina campis). Here the word "sparsaque" provides an explanation for Beethoven's here-and-there tonal excursions in measures 27-40.

In vocal music of the sixteenth, seventeenth, and eighteenth centuries, the Latin verb "spargo" (or "dispergo") and the Italian "spargere"—all meaning "to scatter" or "to disperse"—regularly invited madrigalistic treatment. In the early examples this word was usually "painted" through the use of angular melismas. Later examples—which would have been more likely to provide Beethoven with an awareness of this tradition—often occur in settings of the Magnificat, where, in the line "he scattered the proud in the imagination of their hearts" (dispersit superbos mente cordis sui), the verb "dispersit" never failed to inspire imaginative treatment. The most familiar example occurs in J. S. Bach's

Another apt treatment, somewhat closer to Beethoven's time, is found in C. P. E. Bach's Magnificat, 1749 (Ex. 14).

What is fascinating about the passage in Beethoven's Fourth Piano Concerto with which we are concerned is that the composer is obviously not "setting" the word "sparsaque"—since this is not vocal music wherein the listener will actually hear that word. In this opening tutti of a concerto, the verb "spargere" merely suggests to Beethoven the idea of tossing musical keys in all directions. And how ingenious the result!

At m. 40 the subject is quickly changed. In an instant, F♯ Minor is changed to F♯ Major (which becomes the dominant of B Minor). Beginning *sempre pp*, the next ten measures gradually mount to a *ff*, at which point D Major is established as the dominant of G Major, the home key (Ex. 15, p. 69).

In this antepenultimate area of the introductory tutti, Beethoven's slow move toward the dominant of the home key is just what we would expect. What is of particular interest here are those melodic gestures that occur along the way in the wind instruments in three octaves. These are brief gestures and of a rather pleading, almost urgent nature. What, we ask, inspired these urgent melodic gestures, as the composer gradually builds toward the all-important dominant?

Ex. 13. J. S. Bach. Magnificat, chorus "Fecit potentum," mm. 24-26

Ex. 14. C. P. E. Bach, Magnificat, bass aria "Fecit potentiam," mm. 47-61

Ex. 14 (cont)

Ex. 15. Fourth Piano Concerto, 1st movement, mm. 40-49

Ovid's next line (line 152) begins "Nunc opus est leviore lyra." "Opus est" is an idiomatic Latin expression meaning "to have need" of something. Frank Justus Miller felicitously translates this sentence, "But now I need the gentler touch ... "[8] For this occasion I provide my own gloss: what Orpheus craves at this point is an elevation from the *graviore lyra* to the *leviore lyra*—a lyric outpouring to express the idea of love.

What follows in Beethoven's musical version of Orpheus's *proemium* is the most enthralling and important melodic phrase in the entire first movement of the Fourth Piano Concerto. It is proclaimed *ff* with the dominant seventh-chord in its 4-2 position—i.e., with the unstable seventh degree prominently sounded in the bass (that low C in the bassoons and horns; Ex. 16).

What this ardent outpouring from Ovid's Orpheus is all about, will be troublesome for certain readers: "and I would sing songs about boys beloved by gods ... " (puerosque canamus dilectos superis). This subject requires another digression.

Ex. 16. Mm. 50-60

[8] Loeb-Ovid, 2:75.

### INTERMEZZO: ORPHEUS, "THE AUTHOR OF GREEK LOVE"

As Ovid reinvents the Orpheus myth, he reports that when Orpheus loses his Euridice a second time, he forswears the love of women and now "sings songs about boys beloved by gods." As a result, explains Ovid, Orpheus became the "author" (auctor) of Greek love.

> Ille etiam Thracum populis fuit auctor, amorem
> in teneros transferre mares: citraque iuventam
> aetatis breve ver et primos carpere flores.

(He set the example for the peoples of Thrace of giving his love to tender boys, and enjoying the springtime and first flower of their youth—the translation of Frank Justus Miller.)

This single sentence—lines 83-85 in Book X of Ovid's *Metamorphoses*—not only alludes to the subject of homosexuality, it implies an advocacy of homosexuality. It was so shocking that it became the chief reason why this monument of world literature was so regularly banned.

A revealing example of the contemptuous attitude toward this objectionable sentence in Ovid occurs in C. F. Cramer's translation of the libretto of the Biehl-Naumann *Orpheus und Euridice*. (Beethoven, you will recall, owned a copy of that translation.) In Act II of Biehl's opera,

Prosperina explains to Euridice that Orpheus has gone forth with his lyre to teach all the world about love. Love, says Prosperina, is Orpheus's Muse, which will reward him with love, and that reward will be the return of his Euridice.

In a footnote Cramer explains that Ovid had fashioned his Orpheus somewhat differently, "in the following untranslatable passage." Cramer supplies the infamous lines from Ovid—without translation, to be sure. Here is Cramer's footnote.

> Solche Begriffe hatte Ovid freylich nicht von dem Zwecke der Dichtkunst. Er bildete seinen Sänger sich etwas ähnlicher, in der unübersetzbaren Stelle:
>
> Ille etiam Thracum populis fuit auctor, amorem in teneros transferre mares: citraque iuventam aestats breve ver, & primos carpere flores.   Aetatis breve ver, & primos carpere flores. Ein feiner Orpheus!

Cramer's sarcastic remark, "Ein feiner Orpheus!" (A fine Orpheus!), is another example of the historical reaction to Ovid's revelation of Orpheus as "the author of Greek love."

## THE CONCLUSION OF THE OPENING TUTTI

The penultimate event in Beethoven's opening tutti is this new musical gesture that leaps from one section of the orchestra to another, plummets down through three octaves, and bounces on E♭—that note in the scale that leans so hard on the dominant (Ex. 17).

Ovid had concluded his *proemium* with Orpheus railing about the Bacchantes, those "maidens who are inflamed by unnatural love, and pay the penalty for their lust" (inconcessisque puellas ignibus attonitas, meruisse libidine poenam). Beethoven's witty measures 60-66 seem to express Orpheus's cavalier disdain for the licentious Bacchantes.

Beethoven concludes his opening tutti with a quiet musical return to his short-short-short-long motive, as though to remind us of Orpheus's remark about Jove being the omnipresent influence in his music (Ex. 18.)

## THE SOLO EXPOSITION

The tensions introduced in the opening orchestral tutti of this movement are now made more explicit in the solo exposition. There is already a subtle element of tension in the arrival of the piano, which enters by isolating that ever-disturbing interval of the tritone (Ex. 19 on p. 75).

In this solo exposition Beethoven's important new materials continue to have links to events in Ovid's "Song of Orpheus." As the tonality moves from G Major to D Major, along the way it hovers briefly in the key of B♭ Major (the flat-six degree of the key being approached). Here, *pp* and *espressivo*, we encounter an exquisite passage for the solo instrument that was suggested to an important degree by the expanded range and new sonorities of the six-octave Viennese fortepiano. High in the treble there soars a lovely melodic line. Almost five octaves below, deep in the bass

Ex. 17. Mm. 60-68

Ex.18. Mm. 68-74

Ex. 19. Mm. 74-77

range, this melody is supported by harmonies arpeggiated in gentle waves. The result is a musical texture like nothing ever found in music composed for the five-octave Mozartian instrument (Ex. 20).

Ex. 20. Mm. 105-08

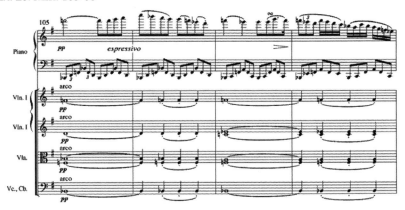

### ORPHEUS'S STORY OF JUPITER AND GANYMEDE (AND THE ILLUSTRATION IN THE GESELLSCHAFT EDITION)

In Ovid's "Song of Orpheus," the musician's first story about "boys beloved by gods" is the one about Jupiter, who has become captivated by the beauty of the Phrygian youth Ganymede. In order to gain this handsome lad as his cup-bearer, Jupiter transforms himself into an eagle. Supported by his broad wings, Ganymede is carried by Jupiter into the sky, sweeping him off to the heights of Mount Olympus. In the illustration in the Gesellschaft edition, as Ganymede is borne aloft, the eagle (Jupiter) peers adoringly at his future cup-bearer (Fig. 13 on p. 76).

In Beethoven's passage, the orchestral strings, also *pp*, provide a harmonic background that employs the short-short-short-long motive but now in gentle rhythmic augmentation. Beethoven's subtle use of rhythmic augmentation at this point is expressive of the image of the mighty Jupiter, transformed by his adoration of Ganymede.

*Jupiter entführet, als Adler, den Ganimed.*

**Fig. 13.** "*Jupiter, métamorphosé en aigle, enlevé Ganimede*" (caption in the Parisian edition, Vol. III, 1769.) Painter Charles Eisen, engraving by Le Mure. "*Jupiter entführet, als Adler, den Ganimed*" (caption in the Viennese Gesellschaft edition, 1791. Engraving by Joseph Gerstner. Department of Printing and Graphic Arts, Houghton Library, Harvard College Library.

The next important event in the tonal plan of this movement is the arrival in D Major, at which point the strings introduce this brief but ardent theme (Ex. 21).

Ex. 21. Mm. 119-22

This theme is peculiar because of what occurs in its second and third measures—a string of ascending leaps: the A moving up to the D, the D up to the F♯, the F♯ up to the B, then the B up to the D—with this D marked *sf!* What could have motivated this odd exercise in melodic ascent? (This rising contour does infuse Beethoven's brief melodic phrase with a sense of ardent enthusiasm.)

### ORPHEUS'S STORY OF APOLLO AND HYACINTH (AND THE ILLUSTRATION IN THE GESELLSCHAFT EDITION)

In Ovid's "Song of Orpheus" the second story about "boys beloved by gods" is the one about the handsome youth Hyacinth, with whom the god Apollo has fallen in love. The two of them sport together, stripping naked, oiling their bodies, and tossing the discus. Apollo hurls the discus high into the air ... but the wind drives the discus off course. As the discus plummets to earth, it strikes Hyacinth on the head, instantly killing him.

Apollo laments the death of his young friend and seeks to honor him by placing him in the sky as a star. (As Ovid later develops this tale, Hyacinth becomes metamorphosed into a flower.) In the illustration in the Gesellschaft edition, Apollo hovers over the figure of Hyacinth with a mixture of adoration and dismay (Fig. 14).

At this point in the story Ovid declares, "And thou, youth of Amyclae [Hyacinth], Phoebus [Apollo] would place in the sky." The poet's Latin words are, "Te quoque, Amyclide, posuisset in aethere Phoebus." A close study of Ovid's sentence and Beethoven's theme reveals an intriguing string of correspondences. We observe that the notes in Beethoven's theme in D Major have strikingly consistent "madrigalistic" relationships to the seven words in Ovid's declarative sentence.

*Hyacinth wird im Spiele mit Apoll von einem
Scheibenwurf getödtet.*

Fig. 14. "*Hyacinthe jouant avec Apollon, meurt d'un coup de palet, que le vent détourna*" (caption in the Parisian edition, Vol. III, 1769). Painter Charles Eisen, engraving by Nicolas Ponce. "*Hÿacinth wird im Spiele mit Apoll von einem Scheibenwurf getödtet*" (caption in the Viennese Gesellschaft edition, 1791.) Engraving by V. Grüner. Department of Printing and Graphic Arts, Houghton Library, Harvard College Library.

To wit, Beethoven's initial half-note stresses the important first two words, "Te quoque" (And thou). The odd sequence of upward leaping intervals—A, D, F♯, B, D—reflects the visual image "posuisset in aethere" (would place in the sky). The two *sf*'s on that repeated high D are a response to the final syllable of Ovid's verb "posuisset" (to place).

As a result, Ovid's emotive sentence can be easily sung, virtually note-for-note, to Beethoven's expressive theme. There is, however, one tiny exception. Whereas Ovid's text contains seventeen syllables, Beethoven's theme involves eighteen notes. Beethoven uses two notes on the first syllable of the word "aethere" (upper air). The early madrigalists had always used the device of a melisma to express the idea of "air," "breeze," or "wind." (Granted, this is as minimal a melisma as can be created—but there it is.)

Some readers will be troubled by the suggestion that Beethoven might have invented a melody on this basis. But in at least two cases we know that Beethoven did do this sort of thing overtly: the opening three notes of his Piano Sonata op. 81a, are a setting of the word "Lebewohl"; the gambit notes of the finale of his String Quartet in F, op. 135, were chosen to fit the words "Muß es sein?" and the reply, "Es muß sein! Es muß sein!" The composition of a melody that will be expressive of specific words is an extremely common and altogether reasonable undertaking. To my ear, what is persuasive in the present case is that Beethoven's D-Major theme so succinctly captures the gentle ardor of Ovid's brief poetic line (Ex. 22).

Ex. 22. Mm. 119-22, texted

A few measures later, in the piano part, we encounter an exuberant passage with this interesting material (Ex. 23).

These measures were suggested by the following passage in Ovid: "Phoebus, well poised, sent the discus flying through the air and cleft the opposite clouds with the heavy iron. Back to the wonted earth after long time it fell, revealing the hurler's skill and manly strength combined." (Quem prius aerias libratum Phoebus in auras misit et oppositas disiecit

pondere nubes; reccidit in solitam longo post tempore terram pondus et
exhibuit iunctam cum viribus artem. Book X, lines 178-81)

Ex. 23. Mm. 127-34

In measures 127 and 129 the rippling chords that surge up from the bass,
over a four-octave range, express the "skill and manly strength" (cum
viribus artem) with which Apollo hurls the discus on high; the long trills
on the high b and the high c♯ in the same two measures then depict the
"long time" (longo tempore) that the discus hovers in the air; and, finally,
those cascading small-note figures in measure 128 and 130 depict the
discus "falling back to the wonted earth" (reccidit in solitam terram).

The concluding events in the solo exposition of this movement (mm. 157-73) never fail to invite comment. In measures 157-60ff. we encounter the return of that ardent *ff* phrase that had first been heard in mm. 50-60 (Ex. 10, pp. 62-63)—that phrase inspired by Ovid's line "and I would sing songs in praise of boys beloved by gods." This time the solo piano adds to the effusion with arpeggiations that sweep through five octaves (Ex. 24).

This builds to a tense, *f* diminished-seventh chord at measure 164, leading us to expect that the central tutti is about to arrive. The protracted trills over the dominant in measures 166-67 assure us that this tutti will arrive at measure 168

Ex. 24. Mm. 157-60

But the tutti does not arrive. The trills continue and the tension deflates. Beethoven now reintroduces the enthralling melody that had first occurred, *ff,* toward the end of the opening tutti (Ex. 10, pp. 62-63). This time, to our amazement, the melody is heard high in the solo instrument, ***pp,*** *dolce e con espressione* (Ex. 25).

The transformation gives this melody the character of a song accompanied by a harp. As Donald Tovey so aptly observed, this passage serves "to reveal the innate tenderness of this majestic theme."[9] With this tenderness Beethoven provides a more sensitive expression of Ovid's line, "Nunc opus est leviore lyra" (now I need the gentler touch). On the several occasions when this theme returns in the progress of this movement, it will become gentler and gentler.

Ex. 25. Mm. 170-73

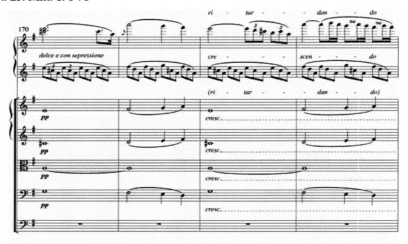

### THE DEVELOPMENT SECTION

The development section of this most inventive concerto movement is remarkable in that—save for the recurring presence of the short-short-short-long "Jove" motive—it ignores all the thematic events that had earlier occurred in both the opening tutti and the solo exposition. Beethoven's development section has a new mission: to thrust us into the important subject of the conflict between Orpheus and the Bacchantes.

At the end of the central tutti Beethoven sets the ground for this new concern by recalling Ex. 17 (p. 73) with its associated text about "maidens inflamed by unnatural love." The development section is launched by the sudden disruption of the key of D Major, with that emphatic f♮ in octaves.

---

[9] Tovey, 78.

This is followed by a return of those disturbing tritones that had earlier introduced the solo exposition (Ex. 26).

Ex. 26. Mm. 192-95

The tonality now slips into the distant field of A♭ Major—the first time in this movement that Beethoven employs a "flat" key. Here, *pp*, Beethoven introduces a new thought: a long descent of eighth-note triplets—a most alluring gesture that he repeats four times (Ex. 27).

Ex.27. Mm. 196-203

Ex. 27 (cont.)

What could have suggested these measures? This passage has to do with that situation of Orpheus and the Bacchantes. Again recall the background: when Orpheus loses Euridice a second time, he foreswears the love of women and then "sets the example for the peoples of Thrace of giving his love to tender boys."

"Still," reports Ovid, "many women [referring to the Bacchantes] felt a passion for the bard" (multas tamen ardor habebat iungere se vati. Book X, lines 81–82). These alluring musical gestures in Ex. 27 were suggested by the scene of the Bacchantes, addressing their "ardor" toward that musician who has forsworn the love of women.

At measure 203, with the deceptive F♯ major dominant-seventh chord marked *fp*, a new tension is suddenly established. In the following musical scramble, as the "allurement" idea (in the strings) dashes from key to key, the fortepiano, with a new musical figure (backed up by the bassoon and oboe), creates an impression of frenzied flight (Ex. 28).This sequence continues for a dozen measures, culminating in music of extreme agitation (Ex. 29).

What inspired this music of pursuit and flight? When Ovid reports, "Still, many women felt a passion for the bard," he immediately adds, "and many grieved for their love repulsed" (multae doluere repulsae). This frenzied episode in the development section (Examples 28 and 29) depicts the Bacchantes expressing their passion for Orpheus, Orpheus fleeing their unwelcome advances, and the Bacchantes exploding in rage.

Ovid, author of the *Ars amatoria* and the *Remedia amoris*, was fond of treating the dismissal of unwelcome amorous advances with mischievous wit. We have no knowledge that Beethoven ever read the *Ars amatoria* or the *Remedia amoris*, but he did read Charlotte Dorothea Biehl's libretto for Naumann's *Orpheus und Euridice*.

Ex. 28: Mm. 204-07

Ex. 29: Mm. 216-26, piano part

Ovid's little drama about Orpheus repelling the unwelcome advances of the Bacchantes was of singular interest to Charlotte Biehl. In Act I, Scene 3 of her libretto, Hersilia, the leader of the Bacchantes, declares to Orpheus, "Ah, for such a long time I have loved you so tenderly!" (Ach, schon so lange, und so zärtlich lieb' ich dich!). "You love me?" reacts Orpheus. "O pain of all pains! Your hatred would give me greater happiness!" (Du liebest mich? O Schmerz der Schmerzen! Dein Haß wär größer Glück für mich!) Whereupon "Hersilia exits in rage" (Hersilia geht wüthend ab).

This exchange has a distinct similarity to the emotional content of the development section in the first movement of Beethoven's Fourth Piano Concerto.

### BEETHOVEN'S REVISIONS OF HIS FOURTH PIANO CONCERTO

In the library of the Gesellschaft der Musikfreunde in Vienna there is a fascinating manuscript of Beethoven's Fourth Piano Concerto (MS A82B) in which the composer recorded an array of revisions in the solo piano part. (These are reported in a valuable recent study by Barry Cooper.[9]) The revisions could have been written down either after Beethoven's first private performance of this concerto in March 1807, or, more likely, after his first public performance of the concerto on December 22, 1808.

These revisions are not corrections. On the contrary, Beethoven wrote them down in order to record several new thoughts. Why these "new thoughts"? Several of them are particularly interesting because of the way they point up details in the work that have to do with his Orphic plan. In the first movement of the original (published) version of this concerto, when the piano reenters at the outset of the development section, its mysterious, questioning tritone had been marked *p* (Ex. 30). In the new-thought revision the tritone is hammered out *f!* (Ex. 31).

Ex. 30: Mm. 192-95 (=Ex. 26 above)

Ex. 31: Mm. 192-94, as revised by Beethoven (Cooper Example 4)

A few measures later we encounter the gesture that depicts the Bacchantes' allurements. In MS A82B the first presentation of this idea is unchanged (Ex. 32).

---

[9] Barry Cooper, "Beethoven's Revisions to His Fourth Piano Concerto," in *Performing Beethoven*, ed. Robin Stowell (Cambridge: Cambridge University Press, 1994), 23-48.

Ex. 32: Mm. 196-97 (= Ex. 17 above)

The second presentation of this phrase, however, is fitted with new articulations in order to make the gesture more pleading (Ex. 33).

Ex. 33: Mm. 198-99, as revised (Cooper Example 5)

The final presentation is then activated with sixteenth-notes (Ex. 34).

Ex. 34: Mm. 202-03, as revised (Cooper, Example 6)

In creating this sequence of progressive changes, Beethoven sought to make this gesture more ardent and seductive.

Then there is the question of Beethoven's alteration of the piano part in measures 204ff. Here, as the Bacchantes (in the strings) continue their pursuit of Orpheus, he flees. In Beethoven's original version of this music of flight, he wrote a long string of closed-position chords arpeggiated over many octaves in sextuplets (Ex. 35).

Ex. 35: Mm. 204-05, original version (=Ex. 28 above)

When Beethoven revised this passage, he abandoned the closed-positioning of these arpeggiated chords. Now he spread out the chords in the right hand of the piano part with open octaves in triplets. These fly up and down over a range of more than three octaves (Ex. 36).

Ex. 36: Mm. 204-05, as revised by Beethoven (Cooper Example 6, continued).

And why? To express Orpheus's flight with increased drive!

As I remarked earlier, Beethoven's "new thoughts" about his Fourth Piano Concerto encountered in the Gesellschaft der Musikfreunde's MS A82B are not corrections. Nor can they be deemed improvements on Beethoven's published score. Their only value lies in the ways they point up (and help to explain) details in Beethoven's Orphic program. His new thoughts here will be of value only to those who are interested in that program.

### THE HOVERING MOMENT IN C♯ MINOR

A strange moment in this development section occurs in measures 227-34. The first measures here are extremely fierce—but then yield to a brief mysterious moment, lyric in nature, and altogether new. This occurs in the remote key of C♯ Minor, which has a tritonic relationship to G major (see Ex. 37).

In terms of "abstract" analysis this moment is obviously very important. One therefore wonders, does this strange event have some meaning in Beethoven's poetic plan? I assume that it must and so shall hazard an explanation that is at least reasonable in terms of the larger flow of the Orphic narrative.

Again I find the explanation in the Biehl-Naumann *Orpheus und Euridice*, Act I, Scene 4. Here, when Hersilia finds herself rejected by Orpheus, she mutters to herself, "Woe to him who scorns my love. Death will threaten him!" (Weh dem Verächter meiner Liebe. Ihm dräut der Tod!)

Many readers will be incredulous about this speculation. What I find teasing, however, is that, if this speculation is correct, then this mysterious hovering in the tritonic key of C♯ Minor in the first movement of Beethoven's Fourth Piano Concerto presages events in the concerto's finale where Orpheus will indeed be threatened with death at the hands of the Bacchantes. In fact, in the finale the Bacchantes will tear Orpheus to pieces.

Ex. 37: Mm. 227-34

### The Arrival of the Recapitulation

The most stunning event in the first movement of a Classical concerto is the arrival of the recapitulation. Usually this moment is marked *f* and, almost without exception, the moment is assigned to the orchestra.[10] An extraordinary departure from convention in Beethoven's Fourth Piano Concerto is that the moment of recapitulation is declared *by the solo instrument*, *ff* (Ex. 38).

At no point in this concerto does Beethoven so dramatically demonstrate the fact that the instrument for which he is composing is much more powerful than any Mozartian fortepiano. The moment is the more striking for the dramatic transformation of that hushed five-measure phrase in the solo instrument with which the concerto had begun—where Orpheus had "tested the many strings of his lyre by strumming them with his thumb." In mm. 253-57 (see Ex. 38) it is as though Beethoven is now declaring, "I am Orpheus, and this is my song!"

---

[10]  The frequently cited exception is Mozart's Piano Concerto in E♭ Major, K. 271, where the orchestra shares this moment with the solo instrument.

Ex. 38. Mm. 253-57

## THE CONTINUATION OF THE RECAPITULATION

In the recapitulation, whereas the sequence of events closely follows the sequence of events in the solo exposition, there is one exception. This occurs in measures 105-11, that passage in B♭ Major, on the way from G Major to D Major (see Ex. 20 above). In the solo exposition the lingering in B♭ Major became an occasion for Beethoven to create music suggestive of the image of Jupiter, transformed into an eagle, and bearing Ganymede off to Mount Olympus on his broad wings. When this music returns in the recapitulation, since there will be no modulation to a second key, this passage now appears in the key of E♭ Major (the sub-mediant of the home key).

Apart from that adjustment for purposes of tonal structure, there are three other changes that find explanation in Ovid's text (Ex. 39).

The melodic line in the right hand of the solo piano part is now rather different—this time a bit more ardent. The left-hand part is no longer replete with eighth-note triplet arpeggiation deep in the bass;

Ex. 39. Mm. 275-80

Ex. 39 (cont.)

instead, the arpeggiations now involve sixteenth-note triplets. In the background the strings again play the short-short-short-long "Jove" motive in augmentation, but now pizzicato with brief rests after each note. the result is a more vivid version of the image of Jupiter, transformed into an eagle, carrying Ganymede off to mount Olympus on his broad wings.

Immediately following this, Beethoven introduces two new measures that express extreme agitation—even anger (Ex. 40).

What are these two new measures about? Here is the scene as reported by Ovid (in the translation of Frank Justus Miller): "Without delay he [Jupiter] cleft in the air on his lyring wings and stole away the Trojan boy, who even now, though against the will of Juno, mingles the nectar, and attends the cups of Jove" (Book X, lines 157-161: qui nunc quoque pocula miscet invitaque Iovi nectar Iunone ministrat). I assume that Beethoven's angry measures 281-82 reflect the jealous resentment of Juno as she observes Jove with Ganymede, that handsome lad for whom her husband "burned with love."

## THE CADENZA

Beethoven composed cadenzas for all his piano concertos. For the first movement of his Fourth Piano Concerto, however, he composed two—

Ex. 40. Mm. 281-82

and even a fragment for a third.[11] The most elaborate of these—the one beginning in 6/8--he called his "first cadenza" (erste Kadenz). Beethoven's other completed cadenza is used rarely; for this one he supplied the cryptic caption "Cadenza (ma senza cadere)." What *did* he mean by this pun, "Cadenza (but without falling)?" And why did he take the trouble to write *two* cadenzas for this movement? The reason is that the familiar cadenza beginning in 6/8 contains a hidden program. When this program is understood, some performers may find this cadenza objectionable and thus turn to Beethoven's alternative "cadenza (but without falling)."

The programmatic nature of this cadenza involves the interactive coming and going of three musical ideas in the manner of a debate. This debate can be understood only if one appreciates the associative meanings of the three ideas based on the context in which they were initially presented.

1. The "Jove" idea—so ubiquitous in this movement—now appears unexpectedly in compound-duple meter. With this new meter, the idea becomes nervous and agitated, gradually subsiding into a quiet musical question (Ex. 41).

Ex. 41. Cadenza, mm. 1-20

---

[11] *Beethoven Werke*, ed., Beethoven-Archiv Bonn (München-Duisberg: G. Henle Verlag), Section VII, vol. 7, Kadenzen zu Klavierkonzerten, ed. Joseph Schmidt-Görg (1967), 21-28. The cadenza with which we are here concerned is on 21-25; and the measure numbers used in my examples are those found in Schmidt-Görg's edition.

Ex. 41 (cont)

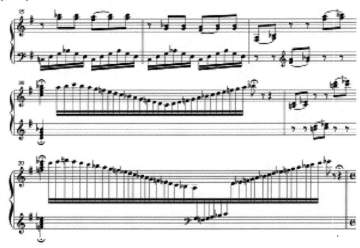

2. The meter returns to common time and Beethoven instructs *Tempo primo*. In B♭ Major, *dolce*, we encounter the melody that reflects Apollo's wish to place his adored Hyacinth in the skies (cf. Exs. 21 and 22 above). This theme is also expanded with a certain unease (Ex. 42).

Ex. 42. Cadenza, mm. 21-35

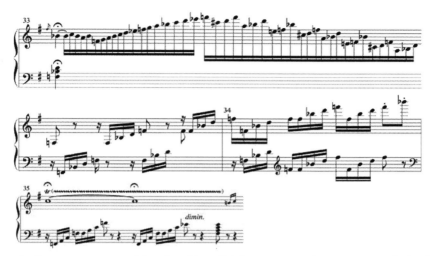

3. In response to this, the "Jove" idea returns (in compound duple meter), now in D Major. In the following measures it thrashes forth with a frenzy—leading to another musical question (Ex. 43).

Ex. 43. Cadenza, mm. 36-48

4. As the "Jove" idea subsides, there emerges, in A♭ Major, that radiant melody so often heard in this movement—the one associated with Orpheus's declaration, "Puerosque canamus dilectos superis" (Ex. 44).

Ex. 44. Cadenza, mm. 74-84

5. This is interrupted by a troubled, two-measure-long recall of the "Jove" idea (Ex. 45).

Ex. 45. Cadenza, mm. 85-86

6. The tonal journey of this cadenza finally brings us back to the home key, G Major. As Beethoven now returns to Orpheus's "Puerosque canamus dilectos superis," the melody soars aloft with a sense of triumph (Ex. 46).

Ex. 46. Mm. 87-100

7.  The debate concluded, Beethoven now attends to the final concern of every cadenza, a preparation for the closing tutti. The closing tutti of the first movement of Beethoven's Fourth Piano Concerto quietly blossoms forth with the composer's consummately tender statement of Orpheus's "And I would sing songs in praise of boys beloved by gods" (Ex. 47 on p. 101).

### Again Regarding "Greek Love"

In their *Beethoven and His Nephew*,[12] Editha and Richard Sterba advanced the eternally controversial assumption that a strand of homosexuality existed in Beethoven's psychological makeup. Maynard Solomon dealt with this sensitive matter by suggesting an alternative explanation:

Perhaps in partial compensation for his fraternal conflicts, Beethoven entered

---

[12] New York: Pantheon, 1954.

Perhaps in partial copensation for his fraternal conflicts, Beethoven entered into intimate assocation with a series of idealized brother figures, This, too, was a continuation of a Bonn pattern, which began with the Breuning brothers, the Romberg cousins, Anton Reicha, Karl August von Malchus, the Kügelgen twins, and others. Typifying the tone of these relationships is Malchus's entry in Beethoven's autograph album upon the composer's departure from Bonn [1792]:

> The heaven of my deep love ties our hearts with bonds which cannot be untied—and only death can sunder them.—Reach out your hand, my beloved, and so until death                    THY MALCHUS[13]

[This is the end of the passage quoted in Solomon's book.]

Similar language is found in a letter from late 1799 or early 1800 written to Beethoven by his cherished friend Karl Amenda, who had returned to Latvia:

> I still approach you with the same heartfelt love and esteem that the value of your heart and of your talent irresistibly and eternally demand of me. You are probably asking how I could have kept at least this assurance from you for so long. Dear friend! O, ask instead how I could ever leave you. Nevertheless, both of these things have taken place; in a kind of stupefaction, I do not know more. Nevertheless, I should not have neglected to maintain your friendship for me in its initial vivacity. What does a poor fellow like me have that could assure me of its continuation? Indeed the value and the assurance of my dearest good are found in itself. You are the one worthy of the most tender and loyal friendship, which I, with all my devotion, will never be able to pay you adequately; and only in your *own* upright heart, the mutual love is found without deserving it, [the love] for me that will continue within it. See, beloved friend! Thus I imagine my relationship with you. Only this conviction enables me to explain the origin and continuation of our bond. If these remarks might appear excessively rapturous to you, I am not in a position to express it more clearly to its fullest and most effective extent. But this must not bother you: you are no normal person! I think that whoever knows you as I do, and only loves you in a normal manner, is unworthy of the divine feeling of love.[14]

Later on in this letter Amenda reports to Beethoven that he has met "a pretty, young, talented Genevan" girl who, "with innocence and tenderness," is in love with him. He seems to suggest that this is a woman whom he might choose when the time came for him to marry. But then he adds that he will cherish memories of Beethoven "even at the hour of my death."

  In early November 1804 Beethoven sent to his friend Stephan von Breuning the gift of a locket that contained a portrait of him by Christian Horneman painted on ivory and dated 1802. This gift was accompanied by a letter. (In this case it is now Beethoven who is revealing his secret emotions.)

---

[13] Solomon, *Beethoven*, 109-11.
[14] *Letters to Beethoven & Other Correspondence*, ed. and trans. Theodore Albrecht, 3 vols. (Lincoln, NE: University of Nebraska Press, 1996), 1:56-58.

Ex. 47. Score, mm. 347-51

Behind this painting, my good dear S[tephan], let us *conceal* forever *what passed between* us for a time. I know that I have wounded *your heart*; but the emotion within me, which you must certainly have detected, has punished me sufficiently for doing so. It was not *malice* which was surging within me against you, no, for in that case I should no longer have been worthy of your friendship. It was passion, both *in your heart* and *in mine*.

But distrust of you began to stir within me. People interfered between us (people who are far from being worthy of *you* or of *me*). Let me tell you that my portrait was always intended for you. You know, of course, that I always meant to give it to someone. To whom could I give it with a warmer heart than to you, faithful, good and noble Steffen.

Forgive me if I hurt you. I myself suffered just as much. When I no longer saw you beside me for such a long time, only then did I realize to the full how dear you were to *my* heart, how dear you ever will be.

Your

Surely you will rush to my *arms* as *trustfully* as you used to do.[15]

There exists no evidence that any of these intense friendships was ever expressed at the physical sexual level. On the other hand, these communications reveal that, on the basis of his own experience, Beethoven understood that friendship between two men can involve deep, intense love. To the degree that such "spiritual" love might have had even the slightest hint of physical eroticism, that would have been a cause for inner conflict. That conflict is certainly evident in Karl Amenda's letter. (Amenda would later marry and become a pastor.)

I believe that the "erste Kadenz" Beethoven composed for the first movement of his Fourth Piano Concerto is a monologue—an internal debate—regarding the emotional and "moral" conflicts associated with the subject of homosexuality. More than that, I believe that this monologue was composed with personal authority since it implies a long history of emotional confusion and conflict.

On the other hand, when Beethoven composed this "erste Kadenz" for his "Orpheus" Concerto—exploring the idea of Greek love, and the conflicting emotions it engenders—he was simply being true to his source: Ovid. Beethoven understood that the theme of Orpheus as "the author of Greek Love" constitutes the central driving force of Ovid's entire Orpheus narrative. Beethoven then realized that this potent dramatic element in Ovid's version of the Orpheus legend could function as a device with which he could link the first and third movements of his Fourth Piano Concerto.

---

[15] Brandenburg, 1:227, letter no. 197; Anderson, 1:118-19, letter no. 98. Many years later, when Beethoven sensed that he was terminally ill and might need to call on the help of trusted friends, he moved into an apartment in Vienna close to the residence of Stephan von Breuning and his wife and son.

## THE CELEBRATION OF THE ORPHIC LYRE

The music that follows the cadenza of the first movement of Beethoven's Fourth Piano Concerto involves three events. The first of these, as we have already observed, is the most exquisite of his sequence of presentations of the "Puerosque canamus dilectos superis" idea. The second event, which follows immediately, is the final statement of the "Jove" idea to remind us, yet again, of Orpheus's declaration that, in his music, the omnipresent influence is Jove. The lengthy tonic pedal point grants this statement an aura of gentle resolution. The third event is a rapturous evocation of the sound of Orpheus's lyre. This experience merits a brief digression.

### INTERMEZZO. ORPHIC INSTRUMENTS THROUGHOUT HISTORY: THE LYRE, THE VIOLIN, THE HARP, THE LYRE-GUITAR, AND THE FORTEPIANO WITH DAMPER PEDAL

When we consider the image of Orpheus and his lyre, what first comes to mind, of course, are those Classical depictions of Orpheus found on the friezes of Greek temples, on frescos in Roman tombs, or on Etruscan vases where he is invarably shown playing his lyre. At several points in later history, however, artists preferred to depict Orpheus performing on other instruments as substitutes for the Orphic lyre. For example, in Italy, in the sixteenth and seventeenth centuries, when the violin was the most exciting new instrument on the musical scene, Orpheus was now almost universally depicted playing that instrument.

In the first years of the nineteenth century the fashionable substitute for the lyre of Orpheus became the lyre-guitar. On pp. 171-72 of this book we will learn that Beethoven instructed his painter friend Willibrord Joseph Mähler to create a portrait of him playing a lyre-guitar. On those same pages we shall encounter Fig. 24, the depiction of a lyre-guitar published in the Leipzig *Allgemeine musikalische Zeitung* in the summer of 1801.

What was particularly fascinating and relevant about the Fourth Piano Concerto, however, was the situation vis-à-vis the harp. The harp had historically been a strictly diatonic instrument. In the mid-eighteenth century, however, it was fitted with chromatic pedals that allowed it to expand its tonal range. It could now join the other instruments of the orchestra; in that context its characteristic sound produced a unique musical experience.

An extremely important event in the long history of the harp occurred on October 5, 1762, in Vienna when the audience at the premiere performance of Gluck's *Orfeo ed Euridice* heard a chromatic harp in the opera theater for the first time. Even before Orpheus sings his first line, it is the very sound of his lyre—*his modern harp*—that causes the Furies to scream in defiance. Says Virgil, "Startled by the strain [of Orpheus's lyre], there came from the lowest realms of Erebus [=Hades] the bodiless phantoms of those bereft of light ... " (at cantu commotae Erebi de sedibus imis umbrae ibant ... *Georgics*, Book IV, lines 471-472.)

One reason why the Infernal Scene in Gluck's *Orfeo* became the most famous scene in opera in the second half of the eighteenth century had to with the contribution of that harp. In 1785 when this opera was performed in Bonn, the fourteen-year-old Beethoven was introduced to the modern chromatic harp. In the following decades "the lyre of Orpheus" was, in fact, the harp.

Charming evidence for this is found in the frontispiece of the volume of Gottlieb Müller's satire of Books 10 and 11 of Ovid's *Metamorphoses* that was published in Vienna in 1807—the same year as the first performance of Beethoven's Fourth Piano Concerto. Here Orpheus is shown garbed in a handsome Empire period suit, playing a harp. (N.B., this is not a modern chromatic harp. It is a smaller, old-fashioned, diatonic instrument known in Vienna at that time as a *Davidsharfe*.)

When Beethoven moved to Vienna in 1792, he became aware that various charlatanistic keyboard musicians were using the fortepiano to imitate the harp. In 1796 he wrote a letter to his friend Johann Andreas Streicher, one of Vienna's most important builders of fortepianos, complaining

> There is no doubt that so far as the manner of playing it is concerned, the fortepiano is still the least studied and developed of all instruments; often one thinks that one is merely listening to a harp. And I am delighted, my dear fellow, that you are one of the few who realize and perceive that, provided one can feel the music, one can also make the pianoforte sing. I hope that the time will come when the harp and the fortepiano will be treated as two entirely different instruments.[16]

It is deliciously ironic to discover that the writer of this letter would, ten years later, compose a piano concerto in which, on the final pages of the first movement, there would occur the most enthralling evocation of the sound of the harp.

What makes this moment wonderfully unique is that Beethoven does not evoke the sound of the harp through the traditional use of arpeggios. Beethoven has his pianist imitate harp-like *glissandos*[17] (Ex. 48 on pages 107-09.)

Then, after the briefest pause comes the explosive question that launches the second movement. Here is the question as worded by Calzabigi:

---

[16] Brandenburg, 1:31-33, letter no. 22; Anderson, 1:25-26, letter no. 18.
[17] This passage owes an important debt to the final pages of the first movement of Mozart's Piano Concerto in C Minor. See my "Cramer, Cramer! We Shall Never be Able To Do Anything Like That!:" Understanding a Favorite Quotation about Mozart's Concerto in C Minor, K. 491, and Mozart's Influence on Beethoven's Concertos," *Beethoven Journal* 15 (2000): 57-63.

Wär es ein altes Weib fürwahr !
Ich raufte nicht ein einzig's Haar
Aus meinen Dichterschädel.

**Fig. 15.** Frontispiece to Gottlieb Müller's *Ovids Verwandlungen Travestiert*, Books 10 and 11 (Vienna: 1807). Courtesy of the Museum der Volkskunde, Vienna.

Chi mai dell'Erebo
fra le caligini
sull'orme d'Ercole
e di Piritòo
conduce il piè?
Here is the question as worded by Kanne:
Hah! Wer wagt es hier zu nah'n?
This is to say that Beethoven's effusive celebration of the Orphic lyre at the
end of the first movement becomes the emotional force that triggers the
second movement.

AN INTERRUPTION, ADDRESSING THE IMPORTANT QUESTION,

WHY DID BEETHOVEN NOT REVEAL AND EXPLAIN

THE ORPHEUS PROGRAM IN HIS FOURTH PIANO CONCERTO?

The reader who has decided not to believe any of the Orphic associations
explained in Chapters Two and Three of this book will want to raise an
important question: if all these things are indeed true, why didn't Beethoven
disclose them? (Incidentally, the reader who, in contrast, has actually chosen
to believe all these things will properly raise this same question.) There are
two reasons for Beethoven's non-disclosure.

Carl Czerny wrote, "It is certain that, in many of his finest works,
Beethoven was inspired by similar visions and images drawn either from
reading or created by his own excited imagination, and that we should
obtain the real key to his compositions and to their performance only
through the thorough knowledge of these circumstances, if this were
always practicable."[18]  Czerny then provides a teasing but revealing
footnote: "[Beethoven] was not very communicative on this subject, except
occasionally when in a confiding humor." Czerny's footnote concludes
with the explanation for Beethoven's reluctance to discuss these matters:
"He knew that music is not always so freely felt by the hearers when a
definitely expressed subject has already fettered their imagination."

This attitude had been set forth a half century earlier by Heinrich
Christoph Koch (1749-1816), who, in the second volume of his *Versuch
einer Anleitung zur Composition*, 1787, delivered an elaborate screed against
"characteristic" music—which, he warned the young musician, was a false
route (an "Abweg") that had become voguish in composition in those
years.

[18] Czerny, 60. In the original original German edition of Czerny's book, this sentence
reads: "Es ist ist gewiß, daß Beethoven sich zu vielen seiner schönsten Werke durch ähn-
liche, aus der Lektüre oder aus der eignen regen Fantasie geschöpfte Visionen und Bilder
begeisterte, und daß wir den wahren Schlüßel zu seinen Compositionen und zu deren
Vortrage durch die sich're Kenntniß dieser Umstände erhalten würden, wenn diese noch
überall möglich wäre."

Ex. 48. Mm. 361-71

Ex. 48 (cont.)

[Certain composers] have sought to produce compositions the characteristic element of which is not a matter of human emotions, but of intellectual trifling ["Spielwerk für den Verstand"]. How, for example, does the composer depict a person in a state of distraction? The characteristic element of his composition exists in rather superficial effects: he links together passages which actually do not belong together; he creates irregular rhythms at points where we assume that the rhythm should be regular; for no good cause he mixes up the minor mode with the major mode—and so forth.

Koch then concludes his diatribe with this amusing story.

What is most comical about the whole business is this. Many such characteristic compositions, heard as examples of pure music [as "bloßes Ideal des Compositions"]—that is, so long as one does not know that they are characteristic—give pleasure. When one hears them as they were actually intended to be heard, however, they displease.[19]

Koch's problem is the one Beethoven (via Czerny) had in mind when he spoke of listeners for whom "music is not so freely felt when a definitely expressed object has fettered their imagination." Koch reports that, on first hearing, he has enjoyed a certain piece of music. When he learns that the piece was composed with some extramusical idea in mind, he is displeased

[19] Heinrich Christoph Koch, *Versuch einer Anleitung zur Composition*, 3 vols. (Leipzig: Böhm, 1782, 1787, 1893), 2:40-42.

since his imagination is now "fettered." And so, as a result of his prejudice, Koch turns against that piece of music which he had originally enjoyed.

(This, obiously, is why Beethoven "was not very communicative on this subject, except occasionally when in a confiding humour.")

Koch refers to this situation as "komisch"—but his disparaging attitude is not just comical, it is historically persistent. In 1966 here is what the Beethoven scholar Joseph Kerman would write about the *Adagio affettuoso ed appassionato* of Beethoven's String Quartet in F Major, op. 18, no. 1. (Beethoven, as we all know, confided to his cherished friend Karl Amenda that this movement had been inspired by the crypt scene in Romeo and Juliet.) Kerman reacts:

> When a composer does start out with too clearly formed an emotional image, and holds to the preconception stubbournly, bending even an impressive technique to its service—what happens in such a case is a different kind of failure. The result is not sentiment, but sentimentality. This is a typical difficulty with Romantic music below the very highest rank, and it is one that manifests itself in the second movement of the Quartet in F. [20]

The other reason for Beethoven's decision not to disclose the fact that his Fourth Piano Concerto, from start to finish, was inspired by the Orpheus legend had to do with  history's problem with the figure of Orpheus—"the author of Greek love." Beethoven respectfully understood that for certain music lovers—past, present, and future—his consistent flow of references to the Orpheus legend would predictably short-circuit their ability to enjoy his concerto.

## THE JOURNEY AHEAD

The next chapter describes a multi-staged musical drama having to do with Orpheus and the Bacchantes. Because of Orpheus's misogyny, the Bacchantes will beat him to death, rip off his head, and toss that head, along with his lyre, into the River Hebrus.

This grisly tale will then lead, however, to a sequence of gratifying outcomes. Orpheus will be reunited with his Euridice. His lyre will be rescued by Jove and soar triumphant, metamorphosed as a constellation in the sky. How will it end? Orpheus's friend Bacchus will punish his sex-crazed minions by metamorphosing then into oak trees, their toes rooted into the ground, and their branches writhing about in torment.

---

[20] Joseph Kerman, *The Beethoven Quartets* (New York: Norton, 1967), 36.

# CHAPTER FOUR
## Music "To Complete the Picturesque Design"
### The Finale of the Fourth Piano Concerto
### ("Orpheus and the Bacchantes")

The third episode in the Orpheus legend is the story of Orpheus and the Bacchantes. This story is told by Ovid, with typically mischievous relish, in Book XI, lines 1-84, of his *Metamorphoses*, beginning

> While with such songs the bard of Thrace drew the trees, held beasts enthralled, and constrained stones to follow him, behold, the crazed women of the Cicones [the Bacchantes], with skins flung over their breasts, saw Orpheus from a hilltop, fitting songs to the striking of his lyre. "Look!" one of them said, "Look! There is the man who scorns us!" ("En!" ait, "En! Hic est nostri contemptor!") (Ex. 49)

From its quiet first measures to the concluding outburst at the end, the finale of Beethoven's Fourth Piano Concerto was inspired by Ovid's story of Orpheus and the Bacchantes—though with occasional borrowings from Virgil, where this story occurs in Book IV of the *Georgics*, lines 520-27. Again some background will be helpful.

### MISOGYNY, AND THE FURY OF THE WOMAN SCORNED, AS SUBJECTS IN ORPHEUS OPERAS

Throughout the history of opera there have been dozens of librettos based on the Orpheus legend.[1] (This is understandable given the nature of the subject.) Virtually all these operas make a point of depicting Orpheus as a musician with magical power and then telling the story of his courageous devotion to his bride Euridice.

Only rarely do Orpheus operas come to grips with the final chapter of the ancient legend: the grisly tale of the dismembering of the musician-hero at the hands of the vindictive Bacchantes. The reason for this omission has to do with the problem of motivation. The Bacchantes destroy Orpheus because he has turned into a misogynist. And how does one deal with *that* in an opera without playing havoc with the image of the heroic lover?

---

[1] See my "The Three Chapters of the Orpheus Legend," 152-70.

Ex. 49. Mm. 1-10

## HAYDN'S *L'ANIMA DEL FILOSOFO, OSSIA ORFEO ED EURIDICE*

In Beethoven's time there was one opera that did touch on this uncomfortable, historically avoided subject: Haydn's *L'anima del filosofo, ossia Orfeo ed Euridice* (composed in London in 1791), the libretto of which was the work of Carlo Francesco Badini. This opera has a strange ending. In the final scene a chorus of Bacchantes suddenly arrives on stage—their first and only appearance in this story. In the ensuing exchange, Orpheus insults the Bacchantes with a misogynistic outburst. (Although this outburst has its origin in Ovid, in Badini's libretto it is ill-motivated and curiously contrived.)

> Chorus of Bacchantes:
> > Vieni, amato Orfeo!
> > Qui dolento star tu vuoi?
> > Deh, consacra i giorni tuoi
> > all—amore ed al piacer.
> >
> > (Come, beloved Orpheus!
> > Why do you wish to remain sorrowful?
> > Ah, devote your time
> > to love and to pleasure.)
> Orpheus (recitative):
> > Perfide, non turbate di più il mio afflitto core!
> > Io rinunzio all—amore e ai piacer de— mortali
> > al vostro sesso imbell*e!*
> >
> > (False temptresses, cease to assail my sorrowing heart!
> > I renounce love, and mortal pleasure
> > addressed to your idiotic sex!)
> One of the Bacchantes, "furiosa":
> > Come? Cosa mai dici?
> >
> > (How is this? What ever have you said?)
> The Chorus of Bacchantes offer Orpheus a cup containing poison:
> > Bevi, bevi in questa tazza,
> > bevi il nettare d'amore.
> > Ti darà questo licore ogni gran felicità.
> >
> > (Drink, drink of this cup,
> > drink the nectar of love.,
> > In this sweet draft all happiness is found.)

He drinks the poison and dies. The Bacchantes launch into a wild frenzy and prepare to tear Orpheus limb from limb ... but a storm suddenly arises. Enormous waves surge onto the scene, and the terrified Bacchantes scream.

> > Oh, che orrore! Oh, che spavento!
> > Oh, che fulmini! Oh, che tuoni!
> > Cento furie in sen mi sento; siam vicine a naufragar.
> >
> > (O, what horror! O, what fear!
> > O, what a whirlwind! O, what thunder!
> > Our hearts are filled with terror! We are about to drown!)

The Bacchantes drown, the tempest recedes, and the curtain falls.

The Badini-Haydn *L'anima del filosofo, ossia Orfeo ed Euridice* was composed for performance at the King's Theater. Rehearsals had only just begun, however, when the production was canceled, I suspect this cancellation occurred when some zealous censor learned that Badini's libretto included a scene depicting Orpheus as a misogynist—the subject that had been historically banned. (The censors in London were almost as strict as those in Vienna.)

Many years later, in 1807, Haydn was able to persuade Breitkopf and Härtel to publish a selection of eleven numbers from this opera. It was only in 1951, however, that *L'anima del filosofo* was first performed.[1]

Whether Haydn shared his abandoned *Orpheus* score with his friend and student Beethoven, or discussed this matter with him, is not known. Three events in Haydn's opera, however, are clear: (1) at the end of Badin's libretto Orpheus reveals himself as a misogynist; (2) for this reason the Bacchantes destroy him; (3) then they, in turn, are killed. Events two and three would later be reflected in the finale of Beethoven's Fourth Piano Concerto.

## BEETHOVEN'S MODUS OPERANDI

In the third movement of this concerto Beethoven works along the same four lines he had employed in the first movement. (1) In the opening pages of the score, a sequence of musical ideas closely reflect a sequence of thoughts that occur at the outset of Ovid's narrative about Orpheus and the Bacchantes; (2) this movement is a rondo, and the important B theme is inspired by the next familiar event in this story: the head of the dismembered Orpheus floating down the River Hebrus, continuing to sing; (3) whereas the finales of most classical concertos use the seven-part rondo form (ABACABA), in this rondo there is no C theme. In its stead, Beethoven composes an extensive development of the A material. This development section is intended to elaborate and intensify the imagery of the Bacchantes' attack; (4) the coda of this movement is the longest coda Beethoven ever composed. Tovey remarks on this.

> The enormous coda (if we take it as beginning after the recapitulation of the second subject [the B/ idea, at measure 299), is exactly five-twelfths of the whole movement, not counting the cadenza.[3]

The enormous length of this "coda" results from the fact that it is based on four progressive events meant to bring the story of Orpheus to a gratifying conclusion. (More of this in due course.)

I shall again focus on the composer's unconventional procedures, and ask why? Again and again the explanations for these unconventional musical events are to be found in a close study of the Latin texts.

---

[2] Florence, May 9, 1951. In this production the role of Euridice was sung by the young Maria Callas.
[3] Tovey, 81.

## THE BACCHANTES' INITIAL ATTEMPT TO DESTROY ORPHEUS

The rondo finale of a classical concerto traditionally begins with a melody introduced by the soloist—in the home key, *p*—then repeated by the full orchestra, *f*. The beginning of the finale of Beethoven's Fourth Piano Concerto reverses this sequence. This rondo launches not with the soloist but with the orchestra—and just the orchestral strings, *pp* (Ex. 49 above).

Czerny described these opening measures as "mysterious." Beethoven's A theme is ten measures long; in this regard, it relates to the five-measure long gestures that had launched the first and second movements. The theme has a sense of hushed tension. "Look!" one of the Bacchantes says, "Look! There is the man who scorns us!"("En!" ait,"En! Hic est nostri contemptor!"). Note those three staccato notes at the  end: the Bacchantes pointing to Orpheus as their *"con-temp-tor!"* In the coda of this movement we shall encounter those three staccato notes performed by the full orchestra *fortissimo!*

Another mysterious aspect of this theme has to do with Beethoven's manipulation of tonality. This movement is in G Major; yet, as is pointed out in every perceptive commentary, the C-major triad that extends through the opening four measures is in fact heard as the tonic of C Major. In the complete phrase this C-major chord will function as the subdominant of G; but Beethoven intends that we should first *perceive* it as the tonic of C. (Later in the movement he will make that intention absolutely clear by approaching the return of this theme via the dominant of C.) Why the C Major here? Ovid explains that the Bacchantes saw Orpheus "from a hilltop" (de vertice cernunt)—and it is from this elevated vantage point that they pounce on the musician. And so, Beethoven ingeniously begins in C Major so that he can then "pounce" onto G Major.

Since Beethoven had launched this movement not with the soloist but with the orchestra, the next ten measures are now assigned to the pianist, who presents the opening ten-measure theme with elegant ornamentation. These ten measures are always explained simply as a variation of the opening theme. The nature of this variation is so peculiar, however, that I prefer to call mm. 11-20 not a "variation" of mm. 1-10, but a "transformation."

The distinction is not just semantic. To be sure, in this movement the many transformations of the A theme are of interest from the purely abstract musical point of view. But then, at some points this A theme will be associated with the behavior of the Bacchantes and at other points with the behavior of Orpheus. It is important to note that this theme does not function as a "symbol" for either of these partners (as is the case with so many leitmotifs in a Wagnerian *Musikdrama*). What is important here are Beethoven's transformations of this theme, since these were created to depict progressive events in the plot.

The pianist's version of the A theme in mm. 11-20 is surely one of Beethoven's cleverest examples of a "transformation." At the outset we observe that in these measures the piano is accompanied by a solo cello (Ex. 50).

The ten-measure melodic phrase in the right hand is blithe in spirit; the pianist's transformation made more cocky by the left hand playing the chords off the beat in every measure, most of them marked with accents.

Ex. 50. Mm.11-20

Ovid reports that the Bacchantes see Orpheus in the meadow below, playing his lyre "fitting his melody to the striking of the strings" (Orphea percussis sociantem carmina nervis). How aptly Beethoven picks up on that word "percussis." (This reminds us of the example in the first movement of this concerto, where Beethoven, in response to Ovid's words "cecini plectro graviore," instructed his orchestral basses to perform pizzicato.)

What occurs in the next eleven measures is totally divorced from musical tradition and can only be explained by a sequence of events in Ovid. One of the Bacchantes "straight off threw her spear at the tuneful mouth of Apollo's bard" (et hastam vatis Apollinei vocalia misit in ora, lines 7-8). (Ex. 51).

Ex. 51. Mm. 21-24

This spear does not wound Orpheus, however (sine vulnere fecit), because he is protected by the magical sound of his lyre. In the next four measures, as the piano repeats the preceding melodic phrase, legato and dolce, the left hand strums a gentle Alberti bass accompaniment (Ex. 52).

Ex. 52. Mm. 25-28

"Another [Bacchante] threw a stone, which, even as it flew through the air, was overcome by the sweet sound of voice and lyre, and fell at his feet" (alterius telum lapis est, qui missus in ipso aere concentu victus vocisque lyraeque ... ante pedes iacuit). (Ex. 53)

Ex. 53. Mm. 29-31

The telescoping phraseology in this opening sequence of events—10, 10, 4, 4, ½ , ½ , ½ , ½ —resembles what Beethoven had done at the beginning of the second movements in the contest between Orpheus and the Furies of Hades. Here in the third movement, how quaint are those flippant notes at the end that so amusingly depict Ovid's image of that stone dropping at Orpheus' feet.

### OVERWHELMING THE PROTECTIVE SOUND OF THE MAGICAL LYRE—"WITH WIND INSTRUMENTS, HORNS, AND DRUMS" (TIBIA, CORNU, TYMPANAQUE)

The Bacchantes now realize that Orpheus is protected by the magical sound of his lyre. Therefore, if they are to succeed in their intent to destroy him, they must first overwhelm his lyre. As Ovid phrases it:

> Cunctaque tela forent cantu  mollita; sed ingenus
> clamor, et inflato Berecynthia tibia cornu,
> tympanaque, plaususque, et Bacchei ululatus
> obstrepuere sono citharae.

(And all their weapons would have been harmless under the spell of song;

but the huge uproar of the Berecyntian flutes, mixed with discordant horns, the drums, and the breast-beatings and howlings of the Bacchanals, drowned the lyre's sound. Lines 15-18, as translated by Frank Justus Miller.)

C. F. Cramer appreciated the importance of these four lines. In the introductory essay to his translation of Dorothea Biehl's *Orpheus und Euridice* libretto, he quoted them in Latin. This passage in Ovid had inspired Dorothea Biehl to write such lines as:

> (Hersilia) Maenads! Sisters! O what disgrace! Feel with me my disgrace! ... Armed with daggers, avenge me!
>
> (Mänaden! Schwestern! O der Schmach! Fühlt mit mir der Schmach! ... ...Dolchbewafnet rächet mir!)

Her minions reply,

> Yes, your shame also strikes at us! Princess, behold! We will avenge you! (Ja, auch uns trift deine Schmach! Fürstin, sieh! Wir rächen dich!).

(Remember, Beethoven owned a copy of this score.)

Hersilia's challenge to her sisters had occurred in Act I of Biehl's libretto. In Act III the Bacchantes burst onto the stage, wielding daggers and threatening Orpheus. Hersilia cries,

> Rise up, comrades, do not spare him! Kill him ten times over! (Auf, Gespielen, kein Verschonen! Zehnfach treff— ihn Tod!)

In Naumann's piano-vocal score this passage is marked *ff*, and the texture of the music makes it clear that at this point the composer has called for trumpets—and probably other wind instruments, and timpani, as well. This is Naumann's response to Ovid's words "tibia cornu tympanaque" (with wind instruments, horns, and drums). (Ex. 54)

Ex. 54. Biehl-Naumann, Orpheus und Euridice, piano-vocal score, p. 103, mm. 1-4

Beethoven's response to Ovid's phrase is even more explosive. Recall that the second movement of this concerto was scored for strings alone. Following that, the first thirty-one measures of the finale were also scored for strings alone. Coming from some five or six minutes of music for strings alone, we encounter the music in Ex. 55! These measures are an even more literal treatment of Ovid's "tibia cornu tympanaque." To create this *ff*, not only does Beethoven bring back the long silent woodwinds and the horns,

Ex. 55. Beethoven, 3rd mvt., mm. 32-41

he calls on two trumpets and a pair of timpani—*instruments now heard for the first time in this entire concerto*. Here is a racket that can drown out the protective sound of Orpheus's lyre. (Only in the first measures of the finale of his Ninth Symphony would Beethoven compose a more jolting *ff*.)

Czerny remarked that Beethoven's Fourth Piano Concerto has a "picturesque design." A picture that would surely have fascinated the composer Beethoven was the illustration of this scene in the 1791 Viennese Gesellschaft edition of Ovid's *Metamorphoses* (Fig. 16 on p. 123).

In this illustration we find Orpheus being attacked by a half dozen bare-breasted Bacchantes hurling branches, spears, and rocks. Orpheus falls back, one arm raised to protect his face, the other arm clutching his lyre. In the sky four birds wildly flap their wings as they escape this mayhem.

The music that follows is a thing of wild attack from the orchestra, and frantic flight on the part of the fortepiano. Music of such vehemence would have been inconceivable on the elegant eighteenth-century five-octave, double-strung fortepiano (an instrument weighing about 150 lbs.); but now Beethoven is composing for the new six-octave, triple-strung piano (an instrument weighing twice as much). These frenzied *ff* passages—which urge the pianist to drive this modern instrument to the hilt—produced the most violent sounds ever heard in a piano concerto (Ex. 56).

Ex. 56. Mm. 53-65

Ex. 56 (cont.)

**FIG. 16.** *"Orphée mis en pieces par les Dames de Thrace, lesquelles furent Métamorpho-sées en arbres de different especes"* (caption in the Parisian edition, Vol. III, 1769). Painter Charles Eisen, engraving by Pierre Charles Baquoy. *"Orpheus wird vonden Bachanten zerissen"* (caption in the Viennese Gesellschaft edition, 1791). Engraving by Joseph Gerstner. Courtesy of the Department of Printing and Graphic Arts, Houghton Library, Harvard College Library.

All this was inspired by Ovid's unbridled, hilarious account of the Bacchantes' wild attack on Orpheus and the terrified musician's attempt to escape.

(Paradoxically, this urgent sense of extreme violence is diminished when Beethoven's Fourth Piano Concerto is performed on a half-ton twentieth-century concert grand. For a pianist to drive such a behemoth to its hilt in this movement would be tastelessly bombastic.)

## THE RONDO B THEME. ORPHEUS'S HEAD, FLOATING DOWN THE RIVER HEBRUS, CONTINUING TO SING "EURIDICE!"

With the arrival in D Major, at measure 80, Beethoven presents this rondo's B theme. Here Beethoven again stands convention on its head. In the usual ABACABA rondo-finale of a classical concerto both the A and B themes are rhythmic and sprightly, even assertive. In welcome contrast the C theme is then lyric and gentle.

In the finale of the Fourth Piano Concerto, however, the lyric, gentle mood occurs with the B theme, an exquisite invention with just two lines of music in the piano. High in the treble range Beethoven floats a new melody. Underneath it the left hand has a slow arch, eight measures long, that rises and falls over a range of two-and-a-half octaves—with the damper rail elevated for the entire passage. (Behind this, a solo cello, in its lowest register, plays a tonic pedal point.) (Ex. 57)

The explanation for this unconventional B theme is found in an ancient story. In Ovid's book XI, lines 50-53, the Bacchantes tear Orpheus limb from limb and toss his head and his lyre into the Hebrus River. The version of this part of the story that Beethoven preferred, however, is the more elaborate earlier account by Virgil.

Whereas it is possible that Beethoven would have been able to read Virgil in the original Latin—in a Latin-German edition published in Vienna in 1802[4]—more likely he worked from the German translation in his own library, where this story is included in Cramer's introduction to the Biehl-Naumann libretto.

> Da noch hat sein Haupt, vom Marmornacken getrennet,
> als im mittelsten Strudel der fluthende Hebrus es wälzte,
> ausgerufen mit kalter Zunge: "Euridice!"
> Ach! mit fliehender Seele: "Euridice!" gerufen;
> "Euridice!" schollen des ganzen Stroms Gestade.

> (Even then his head, plucked from its marble neck,
> as the Hebrus swept and rolled in mid-current,
> with death-cold tongue, called out, "Euridice!"
> Ah! with fleeting breath, called "Euridice!";
> "Euridice!" the banks re-echoed, all down the stream.")
>                                    (*Georgics*, Book IV, lines 520-27)

[4] A six-volume edition of the complete works of Virgil published that year by J. H. Foss.

Ex. 57. Mm. 80-92

In German, the name "Euridice" in pronounced with the accent on the third syllable. (This is also true in the Latin version, "Eurydicen.") This name, therefore, can be comfortably fitted to the soaring melodic line in the first three measures of Beethoven's B theme (Ex. 58.)

Ex. 58. Mm. 80-82

The slow eight-measure arch that rises and falls over a range of two-and-a-half octave in the left-hand part for the fortepiano (with the damper rail elevated) was inspired by the image of the rolling flow of the Hebrus River. (In these measures the unusually wide spacing of the parts for the pianist's right and left hands is reminiscent of Beethoven's use of the same texture in mm. 105-11 and 275-81 of the first movement of this concerto, where the inspiring image portrayed Jupiter and Ganymede soaring through the air, supported by the broad strokes of the eagle's wings.)

In this rondo finale, the B theme is restated by the orchestra, but now in imitative polyphony. The melody is presented by instrument after instrument, sometimes ascending, sometimes descending (see Ex. 59).

Here is Ovid's description of this scene. "As the head of Orpheus floated down the river, mournfully the lifeless tongue murmured, mournfully the banks replied" (flebile lingus murmurat exanimis, respondent flebile ripae, Metamorphoses Book XI, lines 52-53). And here had been Virgil's description. "—Euridice!—the banks re-echoed, all down the stream" (Eurydicen toto referebant flumine ripae, *Georgics* Book IV, line 527). It was through the combination of imagery found in these two versions of the scene that Beethoven arrived at the polyphonic lines in mm. 92-110, "re-echoing" upwards and downwards.

## THE DEVELOPMENT SECTION: THE MAYHEM RESUMED

Just as Beethoven had departed from the conventions of the ABACABA rondo form by creating a B theme surprisingly lyric in character, so, at that point where we might expect the arrival of a new C theme, there is no new theme. Instead, in mm. 200-298, we encounter an extended development section driving from key to key. This music resumes and intensifies the image of attack and flight in Ovid's madcap spirit.

In mm. 221-31 we encounter the first of a number of brief *pp* passages that bring the flute, oboes, and bassoons into the fray, all piping away in their top range (see Ex. 60 on p. 128).

Ex. 59. Mm. 92-110

Ex. 60. Mm. 221-31

Ovid's account of the Bacchantes' dismembering of Orpheus is hilarious: branches, stones, and clods of earth are thrown in all directions, along with the horns of ripped-apart cattle, and more. From this bloody scene, says the poet:

"the first to flee were those innumerable birds who had been attracted by the singing voice of Orpheus." (Ac primum attonitas etiamnum voce canatis innumeras volucres ... Book XI, lines 20-21).

In the 1791 Gesellschaft edition's depiction of this scene (Fig. 16 above), the artist includes several birds darting off in fright. It was this image of fleeing birds that inspired the succession of piping measures in Beethoven's witty development section.

This frenzied development section in the finale of the Fourth Piano Concerto—with its depiction of pursuit and flight—resembles the frenzied development section in the first movement. In the first movement, however, the frenzy had to do with Orpheus's determination to flee the Bacchantes as they sought to seduce him ... and with their rage! In the third movement the frenzy has to do with the Bacchantes' desire for revenge.

## OTHER PECULIARITIES OF THE MUSICAL FORM

The classical rondo form, with its several areas of return, plays havoc with the idea of a consistent narrative—especially with the head of Orpheus coming and going as it does. As I remarked in the last chapter, whereas in this enterprise Beethoven was willing to manipulate classical forms in various unconventional ways, he was not willing to abandon the basic logic of those musical forms.

Because this unusually lengthy development section is closely related to the drama of attack and flight, Beethoven further adjusts the ABACABA rondo form by omitting the expected final return of the A section. The result is a truncated rondo with these elements:

A in G Major (mm. 1-79, including the transition)
B in D Major (mm. 80-159, including the retransition)
A in G Major (beginning at m. 160)
No C. Instead a development of A (extending to m. 298)
B in G Major (beginning at m. 299)
No A. Instead, an extremely lengthy coda (beginning at m. 349, according to Tovey)

Many theorists in our time will take issue with Donald Tovey's use here of the term "coda," finding this a too-simplistic label for 250 measures of music. I separate these 250 measures into four parts and describe each part as a "scene." Each scene is designed to bring the story of Orpheus and the Bacchantes to a gratifying conclusion.

## SCENE ONE: "THE IMPIOUS WOMEN STRUCK HIM DOWN!" (SACRILEGAE PERIMUNT!)

The concluding drama begins at m. 349, where Beethoven changes G Major to G Minor, and then modulates to the field of B♭ Major. There is never an actual cadence in B♭. Rather, there is a remarkable *pp* passage in which the piano caresses harmonies with triplet arpeggios in a high range. Beneath that, the violas, *divisi*, present a new transformation of the A theme, unusual in that it is now so lyric. It is even marked "dolce." This exquisite orchestral texture is like nothing encountered elsewhere in this concerto (Ex. 61).

The passage for the *divisi* violas is poignant and pleading. What inspires it? Orpheus, under attack from the Bacchantes,

> "stretched out his suppliant hands, uttering words then, but never before, unheeded" (tendentemque manus et in illo tempore primum inrita dicentem, Ovid, Book XI, lines 39-40).

Ex. 61. Mm. 366-82 (Orpheus stretches out his suppliant hands, pleading)

The Bacchantes, however, were "moved not one whit by his voice" (nec quicquam voce moventem) (Ex. 62).

Ex. 62. Mm. 383-90 (the Bacchantes are moved not one whit by his voice)

Ex. 62 (cont.)

And so "the impious women struck him down!" (sacrilegae perimunt!), Book XI, lines 40-41 (Ex. 63).

Here is the most striking of Beethoven's many transformations of the A theme. On this occasion he deals with just three notes. As we first heard the theme, those three hushed descending notes at the end—"con-temp-tor!"—had predicted vengeance (mm. 11-12, Ex. 49 on p. 112). The Bacchantes' revenge on their "con-temp-tor" is now unleashed with those same three descending notes, this time hammered out with deadly violence— "per-i-munt!"

### SCENE TWO: ORPHEUS AND EURIDICE REUNITED

This elaborate invention of a three-movement concerto inspired by the Orpheus myth craves resolution. The three most important Roman accounts of the Orpheus legend—Virgil, Ovid, and Hyginus (and Beethoven clearly had studied them all)—are fascinating for the different ways that they conclude this age-old story. Virgil concludes with utter simplicity: the poignant image of Orpheus's head floating down the Hebrus River, singing "Euridice—ah, hapless Euridice!"

Ex. 63. Mm. 391-402 (the impious women struck him down!)

The most winsome sub-plot in the Orpheus legend concerns the musician's love for Euridice and then the double loss of his bride. Historical treatments of the legend frequently display a happy story-book ending, with Orpheus and his Euridice somehow reunited. (Recall the final scenes in the familiar Orpheus operas of Monteverdi and Gluck, both of which honor the operatic convention of the *lieto fine*, the "happy ending." In both operas we find the two loves reunited as a result of divine intervention.)

The poet who first responded to this storybook wish that Orpheus and his Euridice be reunited was none other than Ovid. According to Ovid, following Orpheus's death, "the poet's shade fled beneath the earth and recognized all the places he had seen before; and, seeking through the blessed fields, found Euridice and caught her in his eager arms. Here now side by side they walk; now Orpheus follows her as she precedes, now goes before her, now may safely look back upon his Euridice" (Book XI, lines 61-66).

Beethoven, too, found merit in this reunion. The tenderest episode in his lengthy "coda" involves the return of his B theme, the "Euridice" theme. This important event is carefully prepared. In mm. 459-65 the piano hints at the theme in the strangely remote key of F♯ Major (Ex. 64).

Ex. 64. Mm. 459-65

A few measures later the piano again presents the theme, now in C Major (Ex. 65). (Here, again, is that tritonic relationship.)

Ex. 65, Mm. 466-73

This tonal search can only be a response to Ovid's "seeking through the blessed fields" (quaerensque per arva piorem, Book XI, line 62).

Ovid's next line, line 63, is "[Orpheus] found Euridice and caught her in his eager arms"(invenit Eurydicen cupidisque amplectitur ulnis). At m. 475 Beethoven finally returns to the home key of G Major, whereupon there is a wondrous sense of reunion. "Euridice" is first sung forth by the cellos, then by the violins, then by the entire orchestra (Ex. 66).

### Scene three: Orpheus's Lyre is Transfigured as a Constellation of Stars

In Roman literature one of the most inventive and beautiful conclusions to the Orpheus legend is found in the *Poeticon Astronomicon* by a contemporary of Virgil, Gaius Julius Hyginus (fl. c. 25 B.C.E.). The unifying device in

Ex.66. Mm. 474-95

Hyginus's fascinating mythography is the linking of favorite ancient myths to certain stars and heavenly constellations. According to Hyginus, after the Bacchantes destroyed Orpheus, the Muses approach Jupiter, urging that he rescue this beloved musician's lyre. Jupiter obliges by metamorphosing Orpheus's instrument as a constellation of stars, the constellation "Lyra."

The version of Hyginus most likely to have been available in Vienna to Beethoven at this time was published in Lyons in 1742; in this edition the illustration of Lyra is found on page 505 (Fig. 17).

### POETICON ASTRONOMICON.    505

iifdem , ⁹ quos humeros Eratofthenes fingit , fingulas : in fcapulis ¹⁰ ipfius teftudinis unam : ¹¹ in ima Lyra , quae ut bafis totius videtur , unam.

### VII.

fiani *ejus loci, qui locus eft.* Optime. Vide ad lib. 11. cap. 20. ideoque in textum recepi. Mox *occidere videtur & cum fag.* ediderunt Micyllus ac Schefferus, & ita exaratum in Celeb. d'Orvillii codice.

7 OCCIDERE VIDETUR ] Offendit Modium , quod mox denuo fequitur , *perfpicitur.* Ideo legit : *Haec virgine exoriente occidere , cum fagittario exoriri perfpicitur.* Sed nimirum , non attendit , fequi noftrum genus hoc plebejum locutionis. Vide quae notavi ad Fabul. 16. & 22. SCHEFF.

8 UT BRACHIA SUNT CONJECTA ] Sanctandreana, *collecta.* Nefcio , quid fint *brachia collecta.* Lego *confecta,* & expono per fimplex *facta,* corum , quae funt confecta ut brachia , id eft , ita fabricata , ut hanc fpeciem referant. puto effe clara omnia. SCHEFF. Legerim *collocata.* quanquam Vlitt. 3. habent , *in teftudinem, ut brachia , funt conjectae.* Conjectae Venet. & aliae antiquitus publicatae. MUNCK. Pro *in teftudine* Voff. pr. & Hemft. *in teftudinem.* pro *collecta* Leid. & Voff. fec. *collocata.* Micyllus ac Schefferus ediderunt *conjecta.* ut in Hemft. Voff. pr. & d'Orvill. exaratum eft. pro *quae bum.* Micyll. & Scheff. ediderunt *quas bum.* ut in Voff. pr.

& d'Orvill. fcriptum erat. pro *fingit* Leid. *finxit.*

9 QUAS HUMEROS ] Sanctand. *quas humeros.* Sed *quas* ad ftellas fingulas referri poteft. SCHEFF.

10 TESTUDINIS UNAM ] *Teftudinis duas* ediderunt Micyllus & Schefferus , & duo Vo I. exhibent.

11 IN IMA LYRA] Non improbo quidem. Sed cum Veneta aliaeque antiquiores repraefentent, *in ima lyrae,* videri poffit fcripfiffe *in ima lyrae. Fundum* vocat German. Scholiaftes, *τὰς πέζας* Eratofthenes. Verba Scholiaftae funt, *in fundo unam, in modulo unam.* Lege , *in modiolo unam,* ut in libro Heinfii emendaverat nefcio quis doctus homo. Dictam & *lyram* nomine totius figni ftellam illam , quae in fundo eft, docet nos Proclus, ut & Geminus p. m. 46. Caeterum in fine capitis hujus additur à Veneta & aliis , & *ita omnino funt novem.* Sed MSS. 3. Vlitt. non agnofcunt illa. Difertim alioquin & Eratofthenes, *τὰς πάντας θ'.* Sed decem lyrae ftellas tribuit Hipparchus , octo Timochares apud Theon. in Arat. pag. 37. ed. Lond. MUNCK. Pro *unam* Voff. pr. *una.* Voff. fec. *unam, ita funt novem.*

S s s

Fig. 17: Gaius Julius Hyginus, *Poeticon Astronomicon* (Lugduni Batavorum [Lyons], 1742), p. 505.

It is unlikely that Beethoven was able to consult a copy of Hyginus. In his library was a copy of what was then the best-selling German book on the subject, Johann Elert Bode's *Anleitung zur Kennstnis des gestirnten Himmels.*[5]  In the years 1768-1844 Bode's "Introduction to the Knowledge of the Starry Heavens" was published in ten editions. Assuming that Beethoven acquired his copy of Bode during the years when he was envisioning his Fourth Piano Concerto, the edition he owned would have been the seventh (1801).

Bode's treatise was primarily addressed to astrologers, so there were up-dated calendars in each edition that scientifically traced the orbits of the planets. Bode's descriptions of stars and constellations were equally precise and detailed. For example, he pointed out that the most brilliant star in the northern sky is the bluish-white Vega. On summer evenings Vega is the first star to appear and stands directly overhead. As other stars in the vicinity of Vega come into view, explained Bode, they gradually reveal the constellation "Lyra." (It was during his summer evenings in the villages of Baden and Heiligenstadt that Beethoven became a serious student of planets, stars, and constellations.)

A striking feature of the Fourth Piano Concerto is the fact that so much of the writing for the solo instrument lies so high. The reason is obvious. The fortepianos that Beethoven had known during the first thirty years of his life had a compass of sixty-one notes (i.e., five octaves). The fortepiano for which Beethoven composed his Fourth Piano Concerto, however, now had a compass of seventy-three notes. The twelve new notes were there to provide a sixth octave at the treble end of the keyboard. This new sonic realm became an invitation to new poetic thought. (In our own time, audiences who know Beethoven's Fourth Piano Concerto only through performances on modern pianos, with their eighty-eight note compass, will be fascinated to learn of the composer's excitement as he explored this new musical realm of 1804.)

In the concluding pages of this final movement Beethoven again and again takes his  six-octave  fortepiano soaring into a new realm, celebrating his flights with exquisite evocations of twinkling stars. The following passages in "scene four" of this lengthy coda were inspired by the poetic image of the metamorphosis of Orpheus's lyre as a constellation in the heavens—with the unique brilliance of Vega to steer the flight.

[5] Albert Leitzmann, *Ludwig von Beethoven,* Anhang "Beethoven's Bibliothek," 383, item 34. In his library Beethoven also had a copy of Christoph Sturm's *Betrachtungen über die Werke Gottes im Reiche der Natur und Vorsehung auf alle Tages des Jahres,* 2 vols. (Reutlingen:1811). There are one hunded and seventeen passages in this book that Beethoven marked in the margins, sometimes with one line, sometimes with two, sometimes with three. References to the sun, moon, constellations, planets, and stars are regularly marked with several strokes. See Charles C. Witcombe, "Beethoven's Religion. An English Translation and Analysis of the Composer's Markings in Christoph Sturm's *Betrachtungen,*" M.A. thesis, Dept. of History, San José State Univesity, 1998.

The first hint of this experience occurs in the context of yet another transformation of theme A (Ex. 67).

Ex. 67. Mm. 416-25

The next address of the image—in the aftermath of the cadenza—communicates a sense of urgency: a sequence of trills, first with one voice, then with two, and finally with three voices, rocketing into the sky! (Ex. 68).

Ex. 68. Mm. 500-07

The next version involves another transformation of the A theme—this one marked *leggiermente* (Ex. 69).

Ex. 69. Mm. 520-29

Ex. 69 (cont.)

In measures 546-53 Orpheus's lyre is gently placed in the sky (Ex. 70).

Ex. 70. Mm. 546-53

## SCENE FOUR: BACCHANTES PUNISHED

In contrast to Hyginus's gentle astral imagery, Ovid concludes his version of the story by returning to the Bacchantes.

> However, Lyaeus [Bacchus] did not suffer such crime as this to go unavenged. Grieved at the loss of the bard of his sacred rites [Orpheus], he straightway bound fast all those Thracian women [the Bacchantes], who committed the impious deed, with twisted roots. He prolonged their toes and, in so far as each root followed down, he thrust their tips into the solid earth. And as a bird, when it has caught its foot in the snare which the cunning fowler has set for it, and feels that it is caught, flaps and flutters, but draws its bonds tighter by its struggling, so, as each of these women, fixed firmly in the soil, had stuck fast, with wild affright, but all in vain, she attempted to flee. The tough roots held her, and though she struggled, kept firm their grasp. And when she asked where were her fingers, where her feet, her nails, she saw the bark come creeping up her shapely legs. Striving to smite her thighs with hands of grief, she smote on oak. Her breasts also became of oak; oaken her shoulders. Her arms, you would think, had been changed into long branches—nor would your thought be wrong. (Translation by Frank Justus Miller)

Ovid's madcap imagery inspired Beethoven's last version of his A theme. What had been *pp* is now *ff*. What had been *Vivace* is now *Presto*. And here the basses, cellos, and bassoons thrash about in frenzied triplets. Beethoven's final treatment of theme A was inspired by Ovid's image of the Bacchantes struggling in anguish as their enfuriated leader, Bacchus, metamorphises them into writhing oak trees. As a result, the music that Beethoven had initially created to depict the Bacchantes' determination for revenge is used at the end to depict their punishment (Ex. 71, p. 144).

## THE HUMOROUS CHASTISING OF MALICE ("DIE ZÜCHTIGUNG DER BOSHEIT")

The last pages of Beethoven's Fourth Piano owe a debt to the finale of his Piano Concerto in B♭ Major composed some ten years earlier. That finale is Beethoven's wittiest Turkish rondo. The last pages of the movement present a humorous depiction of the retreat of the terrible Turks over the hills on the far side of the Danube, accompanied by the distant tinkling sounds of the Turkish crescent—the musical instrument in a Turkish marching band that the English dubbed the "jingling johnny."

In Sulzer's *Allgemeine Theorie der schönen Künste* (the article on the "*Lächerlich*" [the laughable]), the author observes that, in the fine arts, the most laughable of all situations has to do with "the chastising of malice"(die Züchtigung der Bosheit). In Vienna, in Beethoven's day, the best known example this was the figure of Osmin in Mozart's popular *Die Entführung aus dem Serail*.

Beethoven's consummate depiction of the "Züchtigung der Bosheit" would occur a decade later in the hilarious romp at the end of the Fourth Piano Concerto. In the aftermath of the punishment of the Bacchantes, the lyre of Orpheus soars triumphant (Ex. 72, p. 145).

Ex. 71. Mm. 568-77

Ex. 72. Mm. 579-600

Ex. 72 (cont.)

## BEETHOVEN'S "NEW THOUGHTS" FOR HIS FINALE

Beethoven's revisions of the piano part for the finale of his Fourth Piano Concerto are fewer than those he provided for the first movement. As regards the relation of these third movement revisions to details in Ovid's narrative, there is one "new thought" that does leap forth. This has to do with the first return of the A theme in Beethoven's rondo form.

Since, in this movement in G Major, Beethoven's A theme so significantly launches in C Major, the composer prepares for the return to C Major with a G major dominant harmony almost thirty measures long (mm. 132-59). He then stretches out the suspense with this cadenza-like flourish for the solo piano (Ex. 73).

Beethoven's "new thought" here is to protract that suspense by the insertion of three peculiar measures (Ex. 74).

And why? The line in Ovid that inspired Beethoven's tense A theme in its initial presentation is not "'Look,' she cried,'Look who scorns us!'" Instead, it is the more emphatic "'Look,' she cried, 'there is the man who scorns us!'" (En, ait, en, hic est nostri contemptor!) With this revision

Ex. 73. M. 159 (Cooper Example 24)

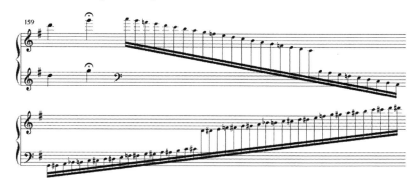

Ex. 74. Mm.159 [159a] and [160] (Cooper Example 24, cont.)

Beethoven prepared the return of the A theme by having the solo piano say, in effect, "Look! Look! L o o k ! (then *pp*) L o o k!"

Such was Beethoven's fascination not only wih the imagery of Ovid and Virgil, but, at certain points, even with those poets' individual words.

CONCLUSION, PART ONE: THE ROLE OF *METAMORPHOSIS* IN OVID, AND THEN IN BEETHOVEN

The reason why the Fourth Piano Concerto has again and again been described as the most poetic of all Beethoven's works is that this concerto, from start to finish, was inspired by the Orpheus legend. This inspiration manifests itself not only in those numerous details but in the very spirit of the work—the way the emotions in the music respond to emotions expressed in the classical texts.

But there is another factor at play here. The central theme of Ovid's enormous compilation of myths is declared in his title, *Metamorphoses* ("transformations," or, in German, "*Verwandlungen*"). These are miraculous transformations, and their purpose is to punish wickedness or reward virtue. In Ovid's Book V, for example, there is the story of Persephone and Ascalaphus. Persephone, Queen of the Underworld, had taken a vow that during her annual trips to earth she would partake of no food. She broke that vow, however, and ate seven seeds of a pomegranate. Ascalaphus saw her do this and remarked on it—whereupon she punished him by metamorphosing him as a screech owl, forever to be shunned as a bird of ill omen (Book V, lines 530-50).

As contrast, in Book VIII we encounter the adorable tale of Philemon and Baucis, a devoted elderly couple who, despite their poverty, extend warm hospitality to two strangers. These strangers turn out to be Jupiter and Mercury, and they reward Philemon and Baucis by metamorphosing them as a pair of beautiful trees that grow so close together that their trunks are forever intertwined (Book VIII, lines 618-724).

Just as the governing process of transformation courses through Ovid's *Metamorphoses*, Beethoven also uses that same process in his Fourth Piano Concerto and in a great variety of ingenious musical ways. Sometimes transformation is expressed in small musical details—as in the first movement, when Jupiter transforms himself into an eagle, and the motive associated with him is transformed via rhythmic augmentation.

Of greater importance are transformations with larger meaning. In the first movement, for example, the "puerosque canamus dilectos superis" theme is initially majestic but then is transformed to reveal its "innate tenderness" (Tovey). This relates to the larger idea that Orpheus starting out as a singer who employs the "graviore lyra" turns into a singer who employs the "leviore lyra." In the second movement Orpheus uses his "leviore lyra" to transform the Furies' anger into compassion.

Beethoven's most elaborate application of the idea of transformation occurs in the third movement, where we encounter those many different uses of his A theme:

- Example 49 (p. 112 above). At the outset this theme is used in association with the Bacchantes' cry, "Look, there is the man who disparages us!"(in those last three notes, their *"con-temp-tor!"*)
- Example 50 (p. 117). Ten measures later, the theme is changed to depict Orpheus out in the meadow "fitting his song to the striking of his lyre."
- Example 55 (p. 120). After a few amusing events, the theme is changed to depict the explosive, overwhelming sounds of combined *"tibia, cornu, timpanaque!"*
- Example 60 (p. 128). Here the theme is charmingly used to depict piping birds escaping the Bacchantes' racket.
- (In the ensuing development section the theme is torn to pieces in response to Ovid's hilarious description of the Bacchantes ripping animals apart and tossing them in all directions.)
- Example 61 (pp. 130-31). The A theme, performed by violas divisi, now depicts Orpheus pleading to the Bacchantes not to destroy him.
- Example 63 (p. 133). The last three notes of the A theme, now *fortissimo*, project Ovid's word *"pe-ri-munt!,"* proclaiming that the Bacchantes have finally succeeded in destroying Orpheus.

- Examples 67-68 (pp. 140 and 141). The theme now gently depicts the several stages of the ascent of Orpheus's lyre, with its final arrival in the stars.
- Example 71 (p. 144). In this thrashing, penultimate version of the A theme, the Bacchantes are hilariously punished.
- Example 72 (p. 145). The Bacchantes punished, the lyre ascends triumphant. Beethoven concludes with resounding applause.

### CONCLUSION, PART TWO: THE LYRE AS ORPHEUS'S COMPANION PROTAGONIST

In regard to the principle of metamorphosis in Beethoven's Fourth Piano Concerto, the sequence of musical events associated with the Orphic lyre is equally fascinating. In measures 1-5 of the opening movement, the lyre is heard in a hushed and tentative manner; in measures 253-57 it becomes enormous and powerful; in measures 347-70 it becomes radiant and triumphant.

In the second movement the lyre assists Orpheus in subduing the Furies of the Underworld, then protects him as he leads Euridice into the world above.

In the finale Orpheus is destroyed by the Bacchantes, but his lyre is rescued and transfigured—as a statement of the triumph of virtue over wickedness. And so we discover that, weaving its way through Beethoven's Fourth Piano Concerto, there is an Ovidian morality play, in which, even as wickedness is punished, victory is granted to the lyre, the symbol of music itself. This "morality play" is delivered through an elaborate array of musical transformations—or *metamorphoses*.

In Beethoven's Fourth Piano Concerto the lyre becomes Orpheus's companion protagonist.

### CONCLUSION, PART THREE: THE WIDER IMPLICATIONS OF BEETHOVEN'S "ORPHEUS" CONCERTO

The many similarities between events in Beethoven's Fourth Piano Concerto and events found in the operas of Gluck, Naumann, and Kanne have already suggested that this concerto was just another work of that period based on the Orpheus legend. Those five illustrations in the Viennese Gesellschaft edition of Ovid's *Verwandlungen* (i.e., *Metamorphoses*) that so obviously and fascinatingly inspired five of the most interesting moments in the concerto advance the case. The countless similarities between events in Beethoven's concerto and events in the texts of Ovid, Virgil, and Hyginus leave no room for doubt. Beethoven's op. 58 is his "Orpheus" Concerto.

The Fourth Piano Concerto is one of the works Czerny had in mind when he wrote (regarding the second movement of the Piano Sonata in C Major, op. 2, no. 3):

In this *Adagio* is already displayed the romantic direction by which Beethoven, at a later period, created a species of composition which carried instrumental music to such a pitch of refinement that it resembled even poetry and painting. In such works we no longer hear the mere expression of feelings, we *see* fine pictures—we *hear* the narration of circumstances. But still, as music, the composition remains beautiful and unconstrained, and those effects are always comprised within the bounds of regular form and consequent development.[6]

Czerny undoubtedly had the same work in mind when he wrote:

It is certain that, in many of his finest works, Beethoven was inspired by visions and images drawn either from reading or created by his excited imagination, and that we should obtain the real key to his compositions and to their performance only through the thorough knowledge of these circumstances, if this were always practicable.

Even as Beethoven's Fourth Piano Concerto was inspired by the Orpheus legend, it also involved an autobiographical metaphor. In this concerto the figure of Orpheus closely resembles the figure of Beethoven. This metaphorical equation is evident in a narrative portrait of Beethoven that was painted by his friend Willbald Joseph Mähler in those months when the three-movement shape of the Fourth Piano Concerto had become clear in the composer's mind.

A close study of the Mähler portrait of Beethoven from ca. 1804 is thus the subject of the next chapter.

[6] Czerny, 36.

# CHAPTER FIVE
*References to Beethoven's "Orpheus" Concerto in the Mähler Portrait, ca. 1804*

## THE MEETING OF BEETHOVEN AND WILLIBRORD JOSEPH MÄHLER

During the years when Beethoven was working on his Fourth Piano Concerto, one of his closest friends in Vienna was Stephan von Breunung. (These two men had been close friends since their boyhood years in Bonn.) In the fall of 1803 Breuning introduced Beethoven to a new friend of his, Willibrord Joseph Mähler. (Mähler came from Ehrenbreitstein on the outskirts of Koblenz, also the birthplace of Beethoven's mother—in other words these three men all came from the Rheinland, and could speak the local dialect.)

> Soon after Beethoven returned from his summer lodgings to his apartment in the theater building [the Theater-an-der-Wien], Mähler, who had then recently arrived in Vienna, was taken thither to be introduced. They found him busily at work finishing the *Eroica* Symphony. After some conversation, at the desire of Mähler to hear him play, Beethoven, instead of beginning an extempore performance, gave his visitors the finale of his new symphony; but at its close, without a pause, he continued in free fantasia for *two hours*, "during all which time," said Mähler to the present author [Thayer], "there was not a measure which was faulty, or did not sound original."[1]

Mähler (1778-1860) was an enthusiastic and capable musician. His initial ambition in life, however, was to be a portrait painter. To this end he had spent the two previous years at the Art School in Dresden. The Akademie der bildenden Künste in Dresden was one of the most important art schools in Europe; the teacher of portrait painting in that school was the widely revered Anton Graff. (Two of Mähler's fellow students during those Dresden years later became the most important early Romantic German painters: Caspar David Friedrich and Phillip Otto Runge.) Mähler had recently moved from Dresden to Vienna to further pursue his training at the art school in that city, where the Director of the Department of Painting was Friedrich Heinrich Füger.

We do not know what communication occurred between Beethoven and Mähler on the subject of portrait painting. But there are

---

[1] Thayer-Forbes, p. 337. Thayer learned this story from Mähler himself.

two things we do know. During Beethoven's early years in Bonn his mentor had been Christian Gottlieb Neefe, who was keenly interested in Johann Georg Sulzer's *Allgemeine Theorie der schönen Künste* and evidently shared that enthusiasm with his young pupil.[2] In Dresden, Mähler's teacher Anton Graff virtually worshipped Sulzer. (Sulzer was, in fact, Graff's father-in-law.)

At some early point in their friendship (in 1804 or 1805) Beethoven asked Mähler to paint a portrait of him. One readily imagines how flattering this request would have been for the aspiring young painter (see Fig. 18).

In the many pages ahead we shall learn that what Beethoven and Mähler achieved together is what Sulzer advocated as a "historisches Porträt"—a narrative portrait or, freely translated, a portrait created to tell a story about the sitter. Mähler's portrait of Beethoven would, in fact, tell *an array of stories* about its sitter. Mähler, coming from the Art School in Vienna—where all the latest ideas in the art world were the talk of the community—was able to share these ideas with Beethoven. But it was Beethoven who master-minded the elaborate plan in this portrait. (The narrative plan in any "historisches Porträt" was always the invention of the sitter.) Beethoven instructed Mähler to do *this* and do *that*—but seems not to have taken time to explain why.

There is no detail in this meticulously invented "historisches Porträt" that does not relate to Beethoven's autobiographical plan. Beethoven expresses this elaborate plan via a series of references to four of his compositions: 1, the *Eroica* Symphony; 2, the "Scene by the Brook" in the *Pastoral* Symphony; 3, the haunting third movement of his Symphony in C Minor; and 4, all three movements of the Fourth Piano Concerto. When Mähler painted his portrait of Beethoven, works 2, 3, and 4 in this plan existed only in their composer's imagination.

In the sketchbook for the *Eroica* Symphony we encounter the germinal thoughts for those three soon-to-be composed works: the "Orpheus" Concerto, op. 58, and the two symphonies, opp. 67 and 68.

## BEETHOVEN AS "GRAND HOMME" (AND THE *EROICA* SYMPHONY)

In the Mähler portrait the most important message is proclaimed via the pose of Beethoven's body. The composer is seated but his body is erect and he leans a bit forward. His weight is on his right leg, his left leg is somewhat behind, giving the impression that the composer is about to leap forward. In the last decades of the eighteenth century—especially in the field of sculpture—this was a canonic pose.

In 1774 Louis XVI decided that the royal art collection should be made accessible to the public, and so he planned to create the greatest art

---

[2] See my "Exploring Sulzer's *Allgemeine Theorie*," 11n12.

**Fig.18.** Willibrord Joseph Mähler, *Ludwig van Beethoven (ca. 1804-1805)*. Courtesy of the Historisches Museum der Stadt Wien.

museum in the world in the Palace of the Louvre. To supervise this project the King appointed Charles Claude de la Billardérie, the Comte d'Angiviller; to oversee the design of the gallery the King appointed Hubert Robert.[3]

[3] James L. Connelly, "The Grand Gallery of the Louvre and the Museum Project," *Journal of the Society of Architectural Historians* 31, no. 1 (March 1972): 120-37.

(Needless to say, news of this stupendous project reached every art school in Europe.) The Comte d'Angiviller, caught up in the spirit of the Enlightenment, decided that there should be installed an array of statues of great French citizens of the time ("grands hommes") on either side of the Grand Gallery.[4]

(Although this project was never completed, no fewer than twenty-nine of the numerous statues that were commissioned were indeed created. These statues were dispersed over the years; a dozen of them were acquired by the Louvre and are now exhibited together in a single hall of the museum's Richelieu Wing.)

In this project the representation of "grands hommes" assumed two forms. Half of these statues were standing figures, depicting admired legislators, orators, and judges. They were to be placed in elevated niches in order to be viewed from below. The other statues depicted their subjects seated; the men represented this way were philosophers, poets, playwrights, scientists, etc. These statues were placed on low pedestals so they could be viewed at a closer, more intimate range. This comparative relationship is made clear in a "projet" for this gallery drawn by Gabriel Jacques de Saint-Aubin (Fig. 19).[5]

According to this plan all these seated figures would be related to one another through the use of various inflections of a pose that had originated in Michelangelo's statue of Moses, ca. 1513-15, in the church of San Pietro in Vincoli in Rome. This famous, majestic statue—which was intended to be part of a stupendous altar complex—depicts Moses holding the tablets on which God has written his Ten Commandments. The prophet is seated but his body is erect, and he leans forward slightly. His right leg is planted forward, and his left leg is thrust behind, as though the man was .about to leap forth with energy, to present to the future nation of Israel the foundations of their religious law (Fig. 20 on p. 156).

PIGALLE'S "VOLTAIRE"—AND THE ENSUING INTERNATIONAL *CAUSE CÉLÈBRE*

A few years before the project of the Grand Gallery in the Louvre was begun, a committee had been established in Paris to commission a statue to honor Voltaire, the most revered philosopher of his time. The sculptor chosen by the committee in charge of this project was Jean Baptiste Pigalle—and the statue Pigalle submitted to the committee already employed Michelangelo's admired pose. However, Pigalle's statue immediately became controversial since the sculptor had depicted Voltaire as an octogenarian nude (Fig. 21

[4] Andrew L. McClellan, "The Politics and Aesthetis of Display: Museums in Paris 1750-1800," *Art History* 7, no. 4 (Dec. 1984): 438-64.
[5] Diderot Salons, ed., *Jean Seznec and Jean Adhémar*, 4 vols. (Oxford: Clarendon Press. 1957-67), 4:300 and figs. 162, 165.

FIG. 19. Gabriel Jacques de Saint-Aubin, *Projets pour les statues de grands hommes* (1776). Courtesy of the Kungliga Biblioteket, Stockholm.

**Fig. 20.** Michelangelo Buonarroti, *Moses* (ca. 1513-1515), Rome, San Pietro in Vincoli. Photograph by Owen Jander.

on p. 158).[6] The scandalized reaction to Pigalle's audacious depiction of Voltaire turned his project into a cause célèbre. Jean-René Gaborit, the Conservateur en Chef of the Department of Sculpture at the Louvre, wrote:

> The nude Voltaire by Pigalle was without doubt the most decried work of the 18th century. Even before it was finished it drew forth so many witty remarks, epigrams, sarcasms, and anathemas that it is difficult to understand how this statue could have been carried through and preserved intact while so many works highly praised at the moment of their appearance have disappeared, destroyed more through indifference than vandalism.[7]

Understandably, a few years later a more dignified statue of Voltaire was commissioned from Jean Antoine Houdon.

In those same years—as the project for the Grand Gallery in the Louvre advanced—similar statues of "grands hommes" were commissioned: e.g., the eminent scientist Georges Louis Leclerc Buffon, Director of the Academy of Science in Paris, in a work by Augustin Pajou, 1776 and the playwright Molière, in a statue by Jean Jacques Caffieri, 1783 (Fig. 22).

Jean-René Gaborit has provided the following information:

> In the early years of the 19th century this series of statues became even more famous. In the Louvre this series had decorated the hall of the Caryatids, where the Institute held its meetings. Then in 1805 these statues were transported to the new meeting room of the Institute "under the Cupola," that is [at the *Academie française*] in the former College of the Four Nations. To the extent that every educated foreigner visiting Paris in those years owed it to himself to obtain admittance to one of the meetings of the Institute, these works were necessarily much seen. It was only toward the middle of the 19th century that they were somewhat forgotten.[8]

In the wake of the Pigalle/Voltaire scandal—and, more important, as a result of d'Angiviller's project for an assemblage of statues of "grands hommes" for the Grand Gallery of the new museum—knowledge of this canonic pose found its way to the attention of teachers and students at the Akademie der bildenden Künste in Dresden. (The same would have been true at the Akademie der bildenden Künste in Vienna.) The student Mähler was doubtless aware of this famous pose, and understood its significance.

How does this inform the ca. 1804 Mähler portrait of Beethoven? When Beethoven asked Mähler to paint a portrait of him, he wanted a portrait that would first of all depict him as the composer of his *Eroica* Symphony. Mähler suggested the use of that canonic pose used for the depiction of "grands hommes." Beethoven liked the idea, since this pose would place him in admirable company.

[6] This controversy is discussed at length in Judith Colton, "From Voltaire to Buffon: Further Observations on Nudity, Heroic and Otherwise," in *Art, the Ape of Nature* (New York: H. N. Abrams, 1981), 531-48.

[7] Jean-Réné Gaborit, *Jean-Baptiste Pigalle, 1714-1785: Sculptures de Musée du Louvre* (Paris: Editions de la Réunion des musées nationaux, 1985), 70-74, esp. 70.

[8] In a communication dated April 15, 2002, for which I am most grateful.

**Fig. 21**. Jean Baptiste Pigalle, "*À Monsieur de Voltaire, par les gens de lettres, ses compatriotes et ses contemporaines—1776,*" Paris, Musée du Louvre. Courtesy of the Réunion des Musées Nationaux.

**Fig. 22**. Jean Jacques Caffieri, *Molière (1783)*, Paris, Musée du Louvre. Courtesy of the Réunion des Musées Nationaux.

In fact, Beethoven liked the idea so well that he described his Symphony in E♭as a work "composta per festeggiare il sovvenire di un gran Uomo." The definition of a "gran Uomo"—or "grand homme"— in the world of late-18th-century French art had nothing to do with military or political figures; it had to do with philosophers, orators, scientists, and playwrights—or, to Beethoven's mind, composers of music.

## THE *EROICA* SYMPHONY: A SYMPHONY "TO CELEBRATE THE RECOLLECTION OF A GREAT MAN"

The title page of its first edition (October 1806) reads:
SINFONIA *EROICA*
. . . composta per festeggiare il sovvenire di un gran Uomo
(composed to celebrate the recollection of a great man).

The title page of the copyist's manuscript, however, had read this way:
Sinfonia Grande
Intitulata Bonaparte
[1804] im August
Del [or de] Sigr.
Louis van Beethoven
Geschrieben
auf Bonaparte
Sinfonia [or Sinfonie] 3 op. 55

Every Beethoven enthusiast is familiar with the story about this title page that was reported by Ferdinand Ries. When Beethoven learned that Napoleon Bonaparte had declared himself emperor, he flew into a rage and shouted,

> So he too is nothing more than an ordinary man. Now he also will trample all human rights underfoot, and only pander to his own ambition. He will place himself above everyone, and become a tyrant!

—whereupon he seized the copyist's manuscript for his new symphony and scratched out the second line on the title page, "Intitulata Bonaparte."[9]

The most trenchant investigation of the problem regarding Beethoven's dedication of his *Eroica* Symphony was accomplished by Maynard Solomon, who explains that Beethoven was always ambivalent, at

---

[9] Franz Gerhard Wegeler and Ferdinand Ries, *Biographische Notizen über Ludwig van Beethoven* (Coblenz: K. Badeker), 58. *Beethoven Remembered: The Biographical Notes of Franz Wegeler and Ferdinand Ries*, trans. and ed. Frederick Noonan (Arlington, Virginia: Great Ocean Publishers, 1987). The mutilated original title page of this symphony—with Napoleon's name almost completely scratched away—is reproduced in H. C. Robbins Landon, comp. and ed., *Beethoven: A Documentary Study* (New York: Macmillan, 1970), 175. Beethoven's original manuscript is lost.

best, in his attitude toward Napoleon.[10] "It is a curious fact, " Solomon points out, "that there is no evidence whatever that Beethoven had anything other than negative feelings toward Bonaparte prior to 1803." How, then, does one explain this dedication?

In the years 1802-09 Beethoven again and again considered a move from Vienna to Paris. Along the way, however, he was concerned as to how he might be received in that city. One suspects that the obsequious dedication of his Sonata for Piano and Violin, op. 47—"To his friend R. Kreutzer, Member of the Conservatory of Music in Paris, First Violinist of the Academy of the Arts and of the Imperial Chamber"—had the intent of wooing this extemely important musician in order that Beethoven might more readily gain recognition by the Parisian musical establishment.[11] (Ironically, Kreutzer seems never to have performed Beethoven's op. 47, and is even said to have spoken of it disparagingly.) One suspects that Beethoven's dedication of his Symphony in E♭Major to Napoleon—France's "First Consul"—was similarly motivated: an opportunistic device to gain entrée in the highest circles of French society.

"The great man," the "recollection" of whom Beethoven intended to "celebrate" in his *Eroica* Symphony was not Napoleon Bonaparte. Rather, this monumental symphony was intended to be a celebration of the larger concept of the hero. To give profound meaning to this celebration—but without publicly revealing the fact—the heroic figure the composer had in mind was Beethoven himself.

## THE RADOUX PORTRAIT OF BEETHOVEN'S GRANDFATHER, BONN, 1773

As Beethoven and Mähler began work on their project, Beethoven drew the young artist's attention to a painting he owned that  portrayed his grandfather, after whom he had been named.[12] This portrait was painted in 1773 in Bonn by an obscure artist, Leopold Radoux. (Radoux was a sculptor and wood-carver in the employ of the court at Bonn, and this is the only painting that has ever been attributed to him. He seems to have created it as a personal favor.) Beethoven was only three years old when his grandfather died; during his childhood years, the Radoux portrait of the senior Ludwig van Beethoven was prominently displayed in the family home. From several accounts we learn that this painting became the composer Beethoven's most cherished possession (Fig. 23). The background of the story told by this portrait is of utmost importance.

Beethoven's grandfather was for many years the Director of Music at the Court in Bonn. To augment his income, on the side he conducted a small business as a dealer in wine. Alas, this man's wife developed an addiction

[10] Solomon, *Beethoven*, 182.
[11] Solomon, on 169-70, cites documentation for Beethoven's intentions regarding the move.
[12] The following pages are based on my "The Radoux Portrait of Beethoven's Grandfather: Its Symbolic Message," *Imago Musicae* 6 (1989): 83-107.

**Fig. 23.** Leopold Radoux, *Ludwig van Beethoven* (the composer Beethoven's grandfather, 1773). Courtesy of the Historisches Museum der Stadt Wien.

to wine. The problem became so severe that it became necessary for the elder Beethoven to commit his wife to an institution in nearby Cologne. This domestic crisis, the great tragedy in the husband's life, haunted him for the rest of his years.

The Radoux portrait of the senior Ludwig van Beethoven contains a four-stage autobiographical plan that functions as a commentary on his tragic life and the manner in which he survived it. It was the grandson's intention that a parallel four-stage autobiographical plan should be structured into Mähler's portrait of him. (In this new narrative portrait the life crisis in question would be the composer's advancing deafness.)

### THE AUTOBIOGRAPHICAL PLAN, STAGE ONE: THE GRANDMOTHER'S FLOWER-DECORATED RIBBON

In the lower left-hand corner of the Radoux portrait there is a broad band of fabric decorated with flowers. This object is a symbol representing the elder Beethoven's ill-fated wife, Maria Joseph Poll. In Germany in that era it was customary that when a young woman accepted a proposal of marriage she would present her future husband with a sample of her skill as an embroidress, in the form of a flower-decorated band.[13] Although the composer Beethoven never met his grandmother, he had learned about her sad story from his mother.

### THE AUTOBIOGRAPHICAL PLAN, STAGE TWO: THE MEANING OF THE PAGE FROM PERGOLESI'S *LA SERVA PADRONA*

In Sulzer's treatise there is a lengthy article on the subject of the symbol, the *Sinnbild*. (A literal translation of that two-syllable German word is helpful: "an image with a meaning.") Sulzer concludes,

> It is thus an important question in portrait painting: how does one invent a symbol, transforming an ordinary object into something that communicates a message?

I call this "Sulzer's Rule"—and there is no better example of this rule than the flower-decorated ribbon in the Radoux portrait. In the pages ahead we shall encounter more than a dozen fascinating examples of Sulzer's Rule. Early in the adventure we shall become aware that a *"Sinnbild"* is not an invention of the painter of a portrait; it is the invention of the sitter. That rule is well demonstrated by the following story:

The jumbled pages of manuscript music held in his left hand by the grandfather Beethoven, show the Italian words "s'è amore, s'è amore ..." (if it's love, if it's love ...) These words, however, are depicted upside down. The inclusion of a text upside down was a common device in portraiture—a device intended not to obscure the text but to invite inquiry (see Fig. 24).

In the last years of the twentieth century the Dutch musicologist Loek Hautus detected that this brief fragment of music came from Giovanni Pergolesi's extremely popular and widely performed intermezzo *La serva padrona* (1733). Shortly before Hautus died, he communicated this discovery to his colleague Jos van der Zanden, who skillfully explored the matter with fascinating results.[14]

---

[13] *Idem*, 96-98, where this custom is discussed in considerable detail.
[14] Jos. van der Zanden, "Out of Love, or Out of Pity? A Musical Message from Louis van Beethoven," *The Beethoven Journal* 15 (2000): 50-56.

**Fig. 24.** Detail of Figure 23.

Van der Zanden's study begins by pointing out that the dimly lit page in the lower left-hand page of this confused jumble of pages already presents a quotation of the bass line in the opening measures of the first page of Pergolesi's score. As for the high-lighted measures with the text "s'è amore ... s'è amore ..."—the passage that caught the attention of Loek Hautus—these occur in an aria in the second act, an aria sung by the character Uberto, a basso buffo.

It is evident that Pergolesi's *La serva padrona* was at some point performed at the Court Theater in Bonn. (A manuscript copy of the score existed in the court library.) Since the grandfather Ludwig van Beethoven was a widely admired basso, the role of Uberto could have been sung by him.

The plot of *La serva padrona* has to do with a conniving servant girl, Serpina, who is determined to get her wealthy but simple-minded master, Uberto, to marry her. In order to make Uberto jealous, Serpina tells him that she has a lover (this is a fiction); for Uberto, this sly plot creates a confusing situation. He sings:

> Son imbrogliato io già!
> Ho un certo che nel core
> Che dir per me non so.
> S'è amore, o s'è pietà?
> Sent'un che poi mi dice,
> "Uberto, pensa a te!"
> Io sto fra il s", e il no,
> E sempre più m'imbroglio.
> Ah, misero infelice!
> Che mai sarà di me?

Idiomatically translated:

> I'm caught in an imbroglio!
> My heart is telling me something ...

But I'm not sure what this is all about.
Is it love, or is it pity?
But I also feel something telling me,
"Uberto, watch out! Think about yourself!"
I stand between "yes" and "no"—
Between "I want to" and "I don't want to."
I am more and more embroiled.
Ah, unhappy wretch!
What ever will come of me?

Uberto's could not decide how should he deal with this problematic woman? What is motivating him? "Is it love?" (s'è amore?), or "is it pity?" (o s'è pietà?). In either case, he should be cautious and take care of himself.

Uberto's predicament was painfully similar to the grandfather Beethoven's own situation. His wife had become a hopeless alcoholic, and he faced the question, how should *he* deal with *this* problematic woman? As we have already learned, his ultimate, desperate solution was to commit his wife to an institution.

### THE AUTOBIOGRAPHICAL PLAN STAGE THREE: THE CAPE OF DIVESTMENT

In the Radoux portrait the next stage in the narrative involves the grandfather's clothing. The elder Beethoven is dressed in a housecoat, and he is wearing a dark cape that is slipping from his shoulder.

In narrative portraits from this era, a cape that falls from the body, or is altogether discarded, served as a symbol representing divestment in its larger sense. In the Radoux portrait, the dark cape slipping from the elder Ludwig van Beethoven's shoulder speaks of this man's divestment from the disaster of his marriage.

### INTERLUDE. DIVESTMENT FROM SORROW ... THEN RESCUING ACTIVITY, IN NISA VILLER'S PORTRAIT OF MLLE CHARLOTTE DU VAL D'OGNES, PARIS, 1801

In 1801 one of the works exhibited at the biennial Salon in Paris was a hauntingly beautiful portrait of a young woman identified by the original owners of this painting as Mlle Charlotte du Val d'Ognes (Fig. 25).

For many generations it was assumed that the painter of this unsigned portrait was Jacques Louis David. A recent study by Margaret A. Oppenheimer reveals that the actual painter was Marie-Denise Villers (1774-1821), known to her friends and patrons as "Nisa."[15]

Oppenheimer points out that it was characteristic of Nisa Villers's portraits that they include narrative details. In Nisa's oeuvre there is no more fascinating example of this process than what we encounter in her portrait of Mlle Charlotte du Val d'Ognes. Here the woman gazes at us

---

[15] Margaret A. Oppenheimer, "Nisa Villers. Née Lemoine (1774-1821)," *Gazette des Beaux-Arts* ser. 6, v. 127 (April 1996): 165-80.

**Figure 25.** Marie-Denise Villers, *Portrait of a Young Lady, said to be Mlle. Charlotte du Val d'Ognes* (Paris, 1801). Courtesy of the New York Metropolitan Museum of Art, Mr. and Mrs. Isaac D. Fletcher Collection, bequest of Isaac D. Fletcher, 1917.

with an expression that is both numb and sad. Directly behind her is a window, the corner pane of which is broken. Through the missing area of this large pane of glass, we view a young couple on a distant parapet. The young woman in this remote scene gazes up adoringly at a tall, elegantly dressed young gentleman—and he returns her gaze. Between the two, draped over the railing, is a red cape which, in its sweep, seems to report an amorous link. (In the history of symbolism, red, being the color of blood, most often represents death—but it is also used to symbolize love.) This scene in the distance speaks of a love affair. The cryptic manner in which the scene is presented invites us—indeed compels us—to inquire about this women's situation. Has her young gentleman died? Or has he deserted her? 1n either case, the inventive metaphor of the broken pane of glass implies a painful separation.

In the composition in the foreground we again find a red cape. Presumably this is the same red cape that had figured in the distant scene on the parapet. If so, it is now tossed over the back of the chair in which the young woman sits. And there the cape hangs limp.

Most important, as this young woman stares toward us with her expression of numb sadness, in her left hand she holds a portfolio and in her right hand she grips a portcrayon. (In portraits of painters in the eighteenth and nineteenth centuries, the portcrayon was standardly used to symbolize draftsmanship—draftsmanship being the painter's fundamental skill.)

In effect, Mlle Charlotte du Val d'Ognes is telling us that her way of dealing with the loss of her gentleman friend has been to channel her emotional energy into her work as an artist. Here is the message so often declared by Goethe, that a person experiencing personal anguish can best rescue himself (or herself) through *Tätigkeit* (activity).[16]

### THE AUTOBIOGRAPHICAL PLAN IN THE RADOUX PORTRAIT, STAGE FOUR: THE MESSAGE BEARING GESTURE. DIVESTMENT AND ACTIVITY

The elder Beethoven's right arm now thrusts from under his dark cape— and the energy of this thrust is accentuated by the tassles on the sleeve, which are shown at a strange, gravity defying angle (see Fig. 23, p. 162).

His right hand, however, points back to the music—and here is the grandfather's message: he rescued himself from the emotional torment of his disastrous marriage by devoting his energy to his activity as a musician. (He was the Director of Music at the Court in Bonn·—and he never remarried.)

Goethe could have been been speaking for Beethoven's grandfather when, in the second book of his *Wilhelm Meister*, in 1829, he wrote:

> Torment of the spirit, encountered either by misfortune or through our own fault: to heal this, the intellect can achieve nothing; common sense, little; the passage of time, much. Determined activity (Entschlossene Tätigkeit), on the other hand, everything!

How interesting! Goethe's message regarding the rescuing power of activity is already expressed in the Radoux portrait of Beethoven's grandfather, which had been painted some sixty years before.

Beethoven took possession of this portrait of his grandfather in 1801. In a  letter to his friend Franz Wegeler in Bonn, the composer described

---

[16] See my "The Radoux Portrait of Beethoven's Grandfather," 99-100.

the symptoms of his encroaching deafness. (The is the first time that Beethoven ever discussed his hearing loss in writing.) Later on in that letter he instructed his friend to have this painting shipped to him in Vienna. In each of the many apartments where Beethoven lived in the following years, he prominently hung this portrait and is reported to have called it to the attention of his guests, to whom he then told stories about his forebear. Obviously he admired his grandfather as a musician; but he honored that man most profoundly because of the way he had dealt with the potentially catastrophic situation in his household. It is understandable that, at a time when the grandson Beethoven was coming to grips with the horrendous tragedy of his own life—his encroaching deafness—he would have wanted to have near him this message-bearing portrait of his grandfather.

Sulzer has a lengthy article on the "Porträt" in which he explains:

> This sort of painting is a powerful means through which the bonds of reverence and love between us and our ancestors are strengthened. This healing influence on the spirit is such that it is as though the deceased were still here with us ... A portrait can make almost as strong an impression on a human being as can the person himself.[17]

How appropriate that these remarks were published in 1774, just one year after Leopold Radoux created his portrait of Beethoven's grandfather.

## BEETHOVEN'S GRAND PLAN FOR HIS AKADEMIE OF DECEMBER 22, 1808: CLUES IN THE *EROICA* SKETCHBOOK (1803), AND IN THE MÄHLER PORTRAIT (CA. 1804)

Even as Beethoven was laboring on the composition of his enormous *Eroica* Symphony—a work that would "celebrate the recollection of a great man"— there came to him the vision of an even more enormous undertaking: an entire concert that would "celebrate the recollection of a great man." This concert came to realization on December 22, 1808, in the Theater an der Wien in Vienna. Five years earlier, in the huge sketchbook for the *Eroica* Symphony (dating from 1803), we encounter germinal thoughts for the three principal works in that concert—and in the same sequence in which those three works would be performed on that occasion.[18]

On p. 96: a sketch for the "Scene by the Brook" in the *Pastoral* Symphony. This sketch is captioned "Murmeln der Bäche" and fitted with the cryptic remark "je größer der Bach, je tiefer der Ton" (the deeper the brook, the deeper the sound). This was the generative thought for the *Pastoral* Symphony.[19]

---

[17] Sulzer, 3:720b.

[18] Rachel Wade, "Beethoven's *Eroica* Smphony," *Fontes Artis Musicae* 24 (1977): 254-89, esp. 266f. Also Gustav Nottebohm, *Zwei Skizzenbücher von Beethoven aus dem Jahren 1791 bis 1803*, ed. Paul Mies (Weisbaden: Dr. Martin Sändig, 1970). Music quotations on 56 (*Pastoral* Symphony), 69 (Fourth Piano Concerto), and 70f (Symphony in C Minor).

See my "The Prophetic Conversation in Beethoven's 'Scene By the Brook,'" *The Musical Quarterly* 77 (1993): 508-59.

On p. 148: a sketch for the first movement of the Fourth Piano Concerto. This sketch is an almost exact presentation of the opening five-measure phrase for the solo piano, where Orpheus quietly tests the strings of his lyre. (As we have already observed, five-measure phrases also occur at the beginnings of the second and third movements.) With this five-measure phrase Beethoven introduces the short-short-short-long motive that would later occur again and again in the first movement of his concerto

*This is one of the two existing sketches for this concerto, the other being the Friskin bifolium.*

On p. 156: a sketch for the third movement of the Symphony in C Minor. Here we are introduced to the composer's four-note "Fate" motive—and in the movement that later materialized Beethoven would use this motive to depict in his music the three symptoms of his encroaching deafness.

On p. 157: the dramatic declaration that launches the first movement of the Symphony in C Minor. "So pocht das Schicksal an die Pforte!" was Beethoven's explanation of these measures: "Thus Fate hammers on the gate!" The sequence of these two sketches suggests that in this symphony the generative movement was the third.

This was a concert in C Major. The *Pastoral* Symphony is in F Major, the key of the subdominant of C. The Fourth Piano Concerto is in G Major, the key of the dominant of C. And the scheme culminates with the dramatic arrival of C Major, approached from C Minor.

These three works, first hinted at in the *Eroica* sketchbook (of 1803), would be visually symbolized in the Mähler portrait a year or two later.

## THE AUTOBIOGRAPHICAL MESSAGE IN THE MÄHLER PORTRAIT, STAGE ONE: THE *POLYGONUM BISTORTA* WITH ITS VANISHING COLOR

The plant that Mähler has painted wth meticulous care in the lower left-hand corner of this portrait (on Beethoven's instruction, to be sure) is the *polygonum bistorta*.[20] Because of its twisted leaves, this plant was commonly known as "knot-weed"; because of its delicate flowers, it was also called "prince's feather." The *polygonum bistorta* is a hardy European genus that proliferates along the banks of streams; it grows to a height of about a foot and a half. The large leaves on the upper stalk are oblong-ovate and twisted (thus "bistorta").

The flowers of this plant are produced in what botanists call an "inflorescence," a cluster of flowers. In this species the inflorescence, a dense cylinder of pink flowers, is 1 ¾ " to 3" long by ½" to ¾" wide. The inflorescence of the *polygonum bistorta* begins flowering at its base, near the stalk, and then flossoms forth from one end to the other. As the tiny flowers

[20] The *polygonum bistorta* is described in Thomas H. Everett, *The New York Botanical Garden Illustrated Encyclopedia of Horticulure*, 10 vols. (New York: Garland Publishers, 1982), 8:2749, col. 2.

go to seed, the pink color gradually disappears, vanishing toward the tip of the inflorescence. Finally, as the inflorescence goes completely to seed its color disappears.[21]

The *polygonum bistorta* in the Mähler portrait has six of these cylindrical clusters. The two at the top are in nearly full flower. The three clusters below have flowers only at the tip. The sixth inflorescence—the drooping one adjacent to the cuff of Beethoven's boot—has gone completely to seed and no longer displays any pink color at all.

This careful depiction of gradually receding color is an ingenious visual metaphor for Beethoven's gradual loss of hearing. We know that Beethoven saw in the fading colors of nature a reflection of his own state of mind. He tells us about this in the *postscriptum* of his Heiligenstadt Testament:

> Yes, that fond hope—which I brought here with me, to be cured to a degree at least—this I must now wholly abandon. As the leaves of autumn fall and are withered—so likewise has my hope been blighted—I leave here—almost as I came—even the high courage—which often inspired me in the beautiful days of summer—has disappeared.

As the nature-loving Beethoven observes leaves "falling" and "withering," he compares this to the "blighting" of the hope that his deafness can be cured—then, ultimately, with the very "disappearance" of that hope. Two or three years later, in Mähler's portrait, this is the depiction of the fading inflorescences of the *polygonum bistorta*. Sulzer's Rule about the invention of message bearing symbols is here again in force.

What has this to do with the Akademie of December 22, 1808? The first work in that concert was the *Pastoral* Symphony. In that symphony's "Scene by the Brook," the sounds of the birds and the brook gradually become inaudible in the development section. As these sounds disappear, Beethoven's tonality sinks from G Major to E♭ Major, to G♭ Major ... *and then to C♭ major*. In his initial sketch for the "Scene by the Brook," in 1803, Beethoven explained, "The deeper the brook, the deeper the sound [read 'tonality']." Just as sinking tonality was to serve as a musical metaphor for the idea of Beethoven's receding ability to hear, so the receding color of the blossoms of the *polygonum bistorta* in the Mähler portrait is a visual metaphor for the same idea.

Note the chronological sequence here: the very first sketch of the *Pastoral* Symphony (with its cryptic caption), 1803; the Mähler portrait, ca. 1804; then the composition of the *Pastoral* Symphony, 1808.

---

[21] For the discussion ahead the reader is urged to seek out a reproduction of this portrait in color. Alas, almost every color reproduction in Beethoven books today is so dark as to be useless for an analysis of symbolic details. The reproduction that best captures these details may be found in H. C. Robbins Landon, *Beethoven*, 183, Figure 126.

## The Autobiographical Message, stage two: the Lyre-Guitar with its Missing Top String

In the Radoux portrait, to the right of the flower-decorated band, there are those pages of manuscript music bearing a cryptic message about the loss of something most precious (the grandfather's wife). In the Mähler portrait, in the same position, there is a strange musical instrument that similarly bears a cyptic message about the loss of something most precious—this time, the composer's hearing. This musical instrument is a lyre-guitar, an instrument in high vogue at the time. The lyre-guitar is, basically, a *guitar*—with the same six strings as the normal guitar. At the turn of the century, however, when Neo-Classicism was all the rage, a species of corrupted guitar was invented with a shape meant to suggest a Greek lyre. Beethoven's introduction to the lyre-guitar would have been an article that had appeared in the Leipzig *Allgemeine musikalische Zeitung* in the summer of 1801: "Some Words Regarding the New French Lyre (the Lyre-Guitarre)." (This article stands as the most valuable description we have of the lyre-guitar.) The anonymous author of this most informative article declares, "This fashionable creation is thus [...] a genuine achievement for culture and for taste" (Fig. 26).[22]

At the turn of the century, ladies of fashion were fond of having themselves portrayed holding this visually elegant instrument. (Professional guitarists, on the other hand, despised the lyre-guitar. When the instrument was held as a guitar should be held, it looked awkward and inelegant; and when a lyre-guitar was held upright—as in all those fashionable portraits—it was a nuisance to play.)

The lyre-guitar in Mähler's portrait of Beethoven is an odd invention like no lyre-guitar that ever existed.[23] Even the shape of the upper frame of this peculiar lyre-guitar is unique. What is most significant is the fact that, whereas every lyre-guitar in the brief history of this voguish instrument had six strings, Beethoven's lyre-guitar has only five. (At the turn of the century a guitar with only five strings would have been unthinkable since it would have been incapable of playing the enormous repertory for the guitar that was composed in that period.)

Another bizarre note in the Mähler portrait is the arrangement of its tuning pins. These are like nothing found on any lyre-guitar known to organology. Lyre-guitars were always fitted with flanged tuning pegs, which could be easily turned by the fingers. This instrument has unflanged tuning pins. These resemble the tuning pins on a piano or harp—pins that

---

[22] "Einige Worte über die neue französische Lyra (Lyre Guitarre)," *Allgemeine musikalishce Zeitung* 3 (Aug. 19, 1801), col. 786-89.

[23] See Stephen Bonner, *The Classic Image: European History and Mnufacture of the Lyre Guitar, 858-1848* (Harlow: Bois de Bologne, 1972).

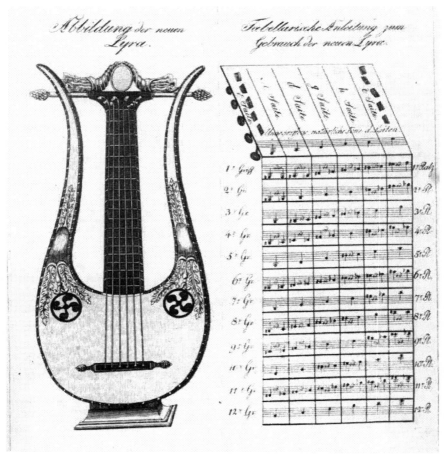

**Fig. 26.** The Lyre-Guitar as Illustrated in *the Leipzig Allgemeine Musikalische Zeitung,* August 9, 1801. Courtesy of the Music Division of the Boston Public Library.

can be turned only with a key. The pins on this instrument are arranged in pairs in a manner similar to what one finds on violins, violas, cellos, and basses, where the lower string of each pair is placed toward the end of the neck of the instrument and the higher string is placed close to the "nut," which is the bridge at the far end of the fingerboard. (Beethoven played both the viola and the violin.)

The purpose of this contrived set of tuning pins is to make it clear that the missing string on this instrument is the string at the top. This reflects Beethoven's report to his friend Wegeler from June 1801, "I can no longer hear the high notes of instruments or voices." Beethoven translated that remark into music in the weird concluding section of the third movement of his Symphony in C Minor—where, in the wind choir, Beethoven's "Fate" motive is passed from one instrument to the next in descending pitch: flute, oboe, clarinet, horn, and bassoon. After each instrument sounds the fateful motive, it disappears. In the aftermath, *pianissississimo*, the short-short-short-long motive then becomes the obsession of the kettle-drum.[24]

Again note the chronological sequence: the letter to Wegeler, 1801; the Mähler portrait, ca. 1804; and the composition of the Symphony in C Minor, 1807-08.

## THE AUTOBIOGRAPHICAL MESSAGE, STAGE THREE: BEETHOVEN'S CAPE OF DIVESTMENT

In the Radoux portrait of Beethoven's grandfather (1773), the sitter's anguish is revealed by the dark cape slipping from his shoulder. In Nisa Villers's portrait of Charlotte du Val d'Ognes (1801), the woman's loss is symbolized by the red cape over the back of the chair on which she sits. In the Mähler portrait of Beethoven (ca. 1804), the sitter reveals his anguish by dropping a dark cape from his body and leaving most of it in a heap on the ground. Along the way, however, in the narrow of Beethoven's back, the lining of his cape reveals a flash of red.

In the Mähler portrait, where this flash of red is the only emphatic use of red in the entire color scheme, Beethoven is clearly alluding to those lurking thoughts of suicide that he had confessed two years earlier in his Heiligenstadt Testament.

Later, in his Symphony in C Minor, Beethoven translated the gloom of his thoughts about suicide into music. This occurs in the bridge from the third movement to the finale—that music with its ominous pounding on the kettle drum beginning with the "Fate" motive. The famous explosion of C Major that launches the finale of Beethoven's Symphony in C Minor is the most powerful declaration of victorious divestment in all of music.

## THE AUTOBIOGRAPHICAL MESSAGE, STAGE FOUR: BEETHOVEN'S GESTURE OF DEFIANCE

In the Mähler portrait of Beethoven the salient event is the composer's extended right arm with its uplifted hand. In narrative portraiture any gesture so centrally positioned, and so prominent as this, is there to deliver a message.

When Alexander Wheelock Thayer was traveling in Europe in 1858 he sought out Willibrord Joseph Mähler—who was then eighty years old—and the two men discussed this Beethoven portrait.[25] (The subject was of special interest to Thayer since he had recently acquired a copy of

---

[24] See my "Let Your Deafness No Longer be a Secret—Even in Art:' Self-Portraiture and the Third Movement of the C Minor Symphony" *Beethoven Forum* 8 (2000): 25-70.

[25] Thayer-Forbes, 337-38.

the painting.[26]) Thayer reports Mähler as describing this gesture, "as if, in a moment of musical enthusiasm, [Beethoven] was beating time." These may have been the elderly Mähler's actual words or this may have been Thayer's own interpretation of this gesture. Whatever the case, "beating time" is certainly *not* what this gesture is about.

In the elaborate vocabulary of message-bearing gestures in eighteenth-century narrative paintings (mythological and historical), one of the most frequently used gestures is the outstretched arm with the elevated hand. This canonic gesture communicates the idea of rejection— even horrified rejection.The gesture was definitively described in Johann Jakob Engel's elaborately illustrated two-volume *Ideen zu einer Mimic*. (Sulzer, in his article "Gebehrden" [gestures], had remarked on the need for a thorough study of this subject[27]—and Engel rose to the challenge.) Engel's treatise, first published in 1785, went through a dozen later editions in five languages.[28] To illustrate the gesture, Engel chose the figure of Medea, who, as she seeks vengeance on her faithless husband, Jason, contemplates the murder of their two sons. In reaction to this thought, Medea thrusts forth her arm and, with hand elevated, cries out, "What a shocking thought! Like the shudder of death it shakes my frame" (Entsetzlicher Gedanke! Wie Schauder des Todes durchbebt er mein Gebein—words quoted from Euripides).

In the narrative painting of Beethoven's day, Engel's "shocking-thought" was encountered on all sides. An example of particular relevance to our present study was an enormous painting exhibited in Vienna in 1802 (Fig. 27). This was the magnum opus of Friedrich Heinrich Füger (1751-1818), the newly appointed Director of the Department of Painting at the Akademie der bildenden Künste in Vienna—and it was apparently as a result of this dramatic painting that Füger received the appointment.[29] As the subject for this virtuosic display piece Füger chose *The Assassination of Julius Caesar*, a scene that would immediately be familiar to every viewer.

Füger's version of this historical scene is consummately theatrical. Sulzer would have applauded Füger's approach since the intense emotions experienced by the men in this scene as they witness the murder of their emperor are expressed by the artist via a spectrum of dramatic gestures.

---

[26] Thayer's copy of the Mähler portrait,, which was done by an unknown artist, is owned by the Music Division of the New York Public Library. In this copy various important details of the original painting are blurred, The copy is reproduced as a frontispiece of the original two-volume edition of Thayer-Forbes. See Luigi Bellofatto and Owen Jander, "A Newly Discovered Portrait of Alexander Wheelock Forbes, by Margarete Auguste Fritze," *The Beethoven Journal*, 21 (2006): "Supplement: Thayer's Copy of the Mähler Portrait of Beeethoven, ca. 1804."

[27] Sulzer, 2: col. 315b.

[28] Engel, *Ideen zu einer Mimic*, 2 vols. (Berlin: August Mylius, 1785-86), 2:198-99. This treatise, primarily addressed to actors and dancers, was also intended to be useful to painters and sculptors.

[29] Walter Wagner, *Die Geschichte der Akademie der Bildenden Künste in Wien* (Vienna: Brüder Rosenbaum, 1967).

**Fig. 27.** Friedrich Heinrich Füger, *The Assassination of Julius Caesar* (Vienna, 1802). Courtesy of the Historisches Museum der Stadt Wien.

In Füger's ingenious plan a half dozen interacting gestures are concentrated at the center of the composition. Brutus, with muscular right arm, raises his dagger, about to thrust it into the neck of his Emperor (who is also his friend). Caesar falls back, crying out, "Et tu, Brute?" At this moment Füger employs Engel's canonic "shocking thought!" gesture—and intensifies it with the device of foreshortening. As Caesar's body falls back, his arm is no longer horizontal but is thrust upward. Since Caesar's hand is now tilted, his fingers are now spread.

In 1803 Mähler moved from Dresden to Vienna to continue his training at the Akademie der bildenden Künste. That year Füger's much admired *The Assassination of Julius Caesar* was very much on display. It can reasonably be assumed that, as Mähler and Beethoven worked together on their project to create a portrait, the artist took the composer over to the Akademie der bildenden Künste to introduce him to Füger's *The Assassination of Julius Caesar* and discuss it.

As regards the technique of foreshortening, the student Mähler was no Füger. Bluntly stated, when it came to foreshortening Mähler was at sea;[30]

[30] See Franz Glück, "W. J. Mählers Beethovenbildnisse und seine Porträte anderer Persönlichkeiten," *Alte und Moderne Kunst* 6, no. 45 (1961). Glück reproduces every painting that has been attributed to Mähler. Most of these are simple half-length portraits of musicians. Besides the ca. 1804 Beethoven portrait, Mähler seems to have done only one other full-length portrait. In none of these is there any element of foreshortening.

and so this gesture, as it occurs in his portrait of Beethoven, makes no impact on the viewer, in whose direction it is aimed. On the other hand, although this conventional gesture is ineptly rendered by Mähler, it is still recognizable. With this gesture Beethoven exclaims, "Entsetzlicher Gedanke!"—and the "shocking thought" is his contemplation of suicide.

### The Reference to the First Movement of the Fourth Piano Concerto: the Lyre of Orpheus

Beethoven's lyre-guitar has two other meanings. First of all, it is a reference to the lyre of Orpheus and thus associates Beethoven with the figure of Orpheus. Then, in this role, the image corresponds to the opening five measures of the Fourth Piano Concerto where Orpheus, with utmost simplicity, tests the tuning of his lyre. (That five-measure phrase, we should recall, had first appeared in the sketchbook for the *Eroica* Symphony, in 1803.) The lyre-guitar is, in short, a reference to the concerto's first movement, "The Song of Orpheus."

### The Reference to the Second Movement of the Fourth Piano Concerto: the Gloomy *Lucus* on the Road to Hades

The second movement of this concerto is the scene in Hades. Virgil tells us that, as Orpheus journeyed to Hades, "he entered a grove that is murky with black terror" (et caligantem nigra formidine lucum ingressus, *Georgics*, Book IV, lines 468-69). A lucus is a grove situated alongside a temple; such a grove was sacred to the memory of the dead. A lucus was traditionally planted with cypress trees, and the light that filtered through these slender conifers created a mysterious atmosphere. In the Mähler portrait, on the left side, there is a classical temple. Alongside this temple we find a pair of cypress trees—and these trees are surrounded by a strange light.

On the distant horizon there is a ruddy glow. I take this to be a suggestion of Hades in the distance. The similarity of these curious details in the Mähler portrait to Virgil's account of Orpheus's journey to the Underworld is suggestive. I assume that with these two details Beethoven is alluding to the second movement of his concerto.

### The Reference to the Finale of the Fourth Piano Concerto: the Writhing Anthropomorphic Oak Tree

In the upper right-hand corner of the Mähler portrait we find a gnarled tree, bare at the top, with a couple of branches that stretch out, left and right, like wildly waving human arms. This tree is patently anthropomorphic.

Regarding this tree, helpful information is provided by Dr. Marie Luise Sternath, research scholar at the Graphische Sammlung Albertina in Vienna.

> The tree in the Mähler portrait of Beethoven has a long history that extends back to the art of landscape painting in the Netherlands; for example, Jacob van Ruisdael. Numerous German landscape painters in the second half of

the 18th century availed themselves of this Dutch "formula." This sort of tree is found with striking frequency in the work of the Dresden landscape painter Christian Wilhelm Ernst Dietrich (1712 Weimar-1774 Dresden) who was a professor at the Akademie der bildenden Künste. In Dietrich's circle, be it among his students or among his friends—and Adrian Zingg was one of his friends—in numerous landscape paintings one encounters this tree with its withered top. The familiar recurring tree in Friedrich's work goes back to this tradition—but now with new symbolic value.[31]

The tree to which Dr. Sternath refers is familiar to every scholar and devotee of the works of Caspar David Friedrich, since it is identifiable in three of that artist's drawings and paintings.[32]

This tree first occurs in a Friedrich drawing dated May 25, 1806 (Fig. 28). The following year, this same tree, minus the stork's nest, was incorporated by Friedrich in a larger composition, a sepia drawing, with three storm-blasted oak trees (Fig. 29). Regarding this drawing, the Friedrich scholar Helmut Börsch-Supan comments, "These oak trees are rendered so precisely that they almost seem to be substitutes for human beings."[33]

Then, in a painting created some fifteen years later, Friedrich again returned to this tree, now using it as the central object in a serene landscape that has variously been titled "Solitary Tree" and "Village Landscape in Morning Light" (Fig. 30, p. 179). (Friedrich himself did not provide a title for this painting.)

Friedrich scholars have discussed this painting at great length in an effort to discern its meaning. The consensus is that this landscape has religious overtones. My own understanding of Friedrich's "Solitary Tree" is that this is a painter's equivalent of what composers over the centuries have called a "tombeau"—a musical tribute to some greatly admired composer who has died. I believe that this profoundly spiritual landscape is Friedrich's "In Memoriam" to Adrian Zingg (1734-1816), who for several decades had been the much-esteemed Professor of Landscape Painting at the Academie der Bildenden Künste in Dresden. In the years 1798-1800, Zingg was Friedrich's most beloved and influential teacher.[34] (Adrian Zingg was presumably among the teachers of Willibrord Joseph Mähler during his three years of study in Dresden.)

[31] In a communication dated October 15, 1999, for which I am most grateful.
[32] Wieland Schmied, *Friedrich,* trans. Russell Stockman (New York: Harry N. Abrams, 1995), 102-04.
[33] Helmut Börsch-Supan, *Caspar David Friedrich*, trans. Sarah Twohig and John William Gabriel (Munich: Prestel-Verlag, 1990), 30.
[34] Useful information about Zingg is found in Ekhart Berckenhagen, *Anton Graff: Leben und Werke* (Berlin: Verlag für Kunstwissenschaft, 1967), 377-79. Graff and Zingg were colleagues at the Dresden Art Academy and were close friends. Graff made several portraits of Zingg; the elaborate one on p. 379 of Berckenhagen's book is Graff's touching tribute to his friend Zingg's stature as a teacher.

**Fig. 28.** Caspar David Friedrich,
*Old Oak with Stork's Nest* (1806).
Courtesy of the Hamburger
Kunsthalle.

**Fig. 29.** Caspar David Friedrich, *Cairn by the Sea* (1806 or 1807). Courtesy of the
Staatliche Kunstsammlungen, Weimar.

**Fig. 30.** Caspar David Friedrich, *Solitary Tree* (ca. 1821). Courtesy of the Staatliche Museen Preußischer Kulturbesitz, Nationalgalerie, Berlin.

When Mähler created his portrait of Beethoven, ca. 1804, he could not have borrowed this tree from Friedrich since his portrait was done earlier than the three works in Figs. 28, 29, and 30. Both Mähler and Friedrich, however, would have had to work from the same model. I assume that this model was a study piece that Adrian Zingg created for his students—though I have had no success in finding such a work.[35]

What is important to our present musical study is the fact that Mähler's tree in the upper right-hand corner of his Beethoven portrait is a crude version of the anthropomorphic tree that would, in later years, figure so importantly in the works of Caspar David Friedrich. In Mähler's Beethoven portrait this tree is even more quaintly anthropomorphic; to wit, Mähler's tree now has a quasi-human face with terrified eyes and a gaping mouth.

[35] Over the years, Zingg produced countless drawings and engravings intended as works that his students could copy. (One of these copies, dated 1799, has survived, since the student in question was the young Caspar David Friedrich, who, like Beethoven, made it a practice to keep such things.) Toward the end of his life, Zingg published three folio volumes of these engravings with titles such as *Studienblätter für Landschaftszeichner* and *Erste Anfangsgründe für Landschaftszeichner: Pflanzen, Baüme, und Feisen*. Since these folio volumes were unbound, they were irresistible to art dealers, who sold the engravings one by one. As a result, no complete sets are known to exist.

Because this area in Mähler's canvas is very dark, these details are difficult to detect in a photograph. The reproduction of this portrait that best captures these details is found in H. C. Robbins Landon, *Beethoven*, p. 183, illustration 126. (See fn. 21 above.) If the upper-right corner of this page is viewed closely (using a magnifying glass), Mähler's grotesque, quasi-human face—with its staring eyes and gaping mouth—is perfectly clear.

How does one account for these strange details? In Chapter 4 we learned how Ovid had concluded his version of the Orpheus legend with a description of the scene of Bacchus punishing his Bacchantes for their slaughter of his friend Orpheus. The punishment occurred via metamorphosis: the Bacchantes transformed into writhing oak trees. The final lines of Ovid's expansive version of the Orpheus legend are again relevant.

> ... each of these women, fixed firmly in the soil, had stuck fast, with wild afright, but all in vain she tempted to flee. The tough roots held her, and though she struggled, kept firm their grasp. And when she asked, where were her fingers, where her feet, her nails, she saw the bark come creeping up her shapely legs. Striving to smite her thighs with hands of grief, she smote on oak. Her breasts also became of oak; oaken her shoulders. Her arms you would think had been changed into long branches—nor would your thought be wrong.[36]

Even as Beethoven involved Mähler in the project of creating a portrait of him—at which time his Fourth Piano Concerto was still in the initial stages of genesis—in the upper right-hand corner of this portrait he and Mähler tucked this Ovidian image of the writhing Bacchante with toes rooted into the ground. (On the bank below Mähler's tormented oak, there also seems to be the suggestion of a foot rooted in the ground.) The grotesque image that we encounter in the upper right-hand corner of this portrait has to do with the frenzied Presto with which Beethoven would later conclude the finale of his Fourth Piano Concerto—with the bass strings and bassoons thrashing about in eighth-note triplets.

## IN SUM: TWO PARALLEL NARRATIVE PLANS

The symbolic plans of the Radoux and Mähler portraits are parallel in their layout. Both portraits employ a circle of narrative elements that move counter-clockwise in five stages. Here is what had occurred in the Radoux portrait (see p. 162).

1. In the lower left hand corner is that strip of fabric decorated with flowers symbolizing the grandfather's bride at the time of their engagement (and also recalling the happy early years of their marriage).

2. To the right of this is the musical manuscript with its cryptic question, "*Sè amore, sè amore*" (in the Italian libretto "*S'è amore, s'è amore*"),

---

[36] *Metamorphoses*, Book XI, lines 76-84; translation by Frank Justus Miller.

representing the story of the grandfather's loss of his wife to severe alcoholism.

3. The circle of symbols next leads to the dark cape, slipping from the man's shoulder, reporting his emotional divestment from tragedy.

4. The circle continues with the arm emerging from under the cape. This emphatic gesture reports the man's escape from his disastrous marriage.

5. As the final event, the pointing hand and finger brings a return to the musical manuscript, which now delivers a double meaning. Originally this object had told of loss. Now the manuscript symbolizes music itself—revealing that it was music that provided this man's route to rescue.

In the Mähler portrait of Beethoven (see p. 153), the conventional pose of the musician's body declares him as a member of the community of "grands hommes." (This relates to the *Eroica* Symphony.) Surrounding that central image is a counter-clockwise flow of symbolic details strikingly similar to those encountered in the portrait of the grandfather.

1. In the lower left-hand corner is the *polygonum bistorta*, with its fading flowers. (This relates to the "Scene by the Brook" in the *Pastoral* Symphony.)

2. To the right of this plant is the lyre-guitar with its missing top string. (This relates to the third movement of the Symphony in C Minor.)

3. A very dark cape slips from Beethoven's body. Even as this cape falls to the ground, at the small of the composer's back it reveals a flash of red—symbolizing his contemplation of suicide. (This relates to the bridge following the third movement of the Symphony in C Minor.)

4. Beethoven's right arm is extended, and his right hand is elevated, with the fingers spread. The man thrusts this hand in the direction of the viewer. This canonic gesture expresses his reaction to a dreadful thought. (This relates to the explosion of C Major at the arrival of the finale of the Symphony in C Minor.)

5. With his left hand Beethoven draws forth his lyre-guitar—now symbolic of the very idea of music. "Nur Sie, die Kunst, sie hielt mich zurück!" (Only you, Art, you held me back!)

On the fringe of this circle of narrative references to the *Eroica* Symphony, the *Pastoral* Symphony, and the C Minor Symphony—symphonies still waiting to be realized—Beethoven then tucked in references to the second and third movements of his "Orpheus" Concerto. These three works—opp. 58, 67, and 68—were envisioned as the structural elements of an awesome autobiographical plan.

## REFLECTIONS REGARDING NARRATIVE PORTRAITS

Why, we ask, do painters and their sitters not provide explanations of their narrative portraits? There are two reasons. First of all, to provide explanations of these symbolic devices would rob them of their intended function, which is to communicate visually without having to resort to words. (Cryptic words, such as the grandfather's upside-down "Sè amore ... sè amore ..." are an exception that merely underscores this rule since these words pose an unanswered question.) Secondly, it is important that the meanings of these symbolic objects not be immediately apparent. The viewer is required to decode these objects. The challenge of decoding, however, can only be met through inquiry into the life of the sitter. Ergo, the ultimate purpose of a narrative portrait is to induce such inquiry. The ideal narrative portrait reveals the sitter to be a model of courage and achievement.

## THE LATER HISTORY OF THE MÄHLER PORTRAIT

Regarding the history of Mähler's portrait of Beethoven, we have only three scraps of information. In a letter from Beethoven to his artist friend, ca. 1804, we learn that Beethoven had lent this portrait to a female visitor during her brief stay in Vienna. Beethoven was anticipating some monetary reward for this favor and promised to share that reward with Mähler.[37]

Then Anton Schindler, in a section of his biography entitled "Beethoven portraits," mentions this painting briefly, adding that, "because of its mediocrity it was never reproduced."[38] This suggests that Beethoven had originally intended that the Mähler portrait would be published as an engraving, so that he (and Mähler, too, perhaps) could gain profit from the thriving contemporary market for engraved portraits of famous composers. If that was Beethoven's original intent, however, he changed his mind.

The reason for this change of mind is provided in Gerhard von Breuning's detailed description of the apartment in which Beethoven lived at the end of his life. In this apartment the Radoux portrait of Beethoven's grandfather was prominently displayed in the entrance hall at the top of the stairs. In contrast, the Mähler portrait of Beethoven himself was hidden away in a small room where, in great disarray, Beethoven stored his manuscripts and his sketchbooks. This room, reports Gerhard von Breuning, "was hardly ever entered by anyone." On the back wall of this storage room Beethoven hung the Mähler portrait—located so that none would ever view it.[39]

Beethoven's decision not to publish the Mähler portrait but rather to conceal it had to do with that story of the dark cape that falls from the body. Once Beethoven had come to grips with the inevitability of his deafness, he wisely chose to divest himself of his earlier anguish. Beethoven's decision

---

[37] Anderson, 1:125, letter no. 107; Brandenburg 1:236-37, letter no. 206.
[38] Schindler-MacArdle,451.
[39] Gerhard von Breuning, *Memories of Beethoven*, ed. Maynard Solomon (Cambridge: Cambridge University Press, 1992), 60-66. On p. 62, Solomon includes a plan of Beethoven's apartment. The room in question is numbered IV. (Solomon's identification "music room" is misleading. This was merely a storage room.)

to hide the Mähler portrait—and along with it, all the elaborate symbolic messages it contained—became one more step that the composer took in putting the agony of his deafness behind him.

What was essential for Beethoven was the spiritually healthy exercise of divestment. In a secret compartment of a piece of furniture in his final dwelling, Beethoven hid his Heiligenstadt Testament—thus divesting himself of the agony it reported. In that same dwelling on the back wall of a storage room, he hid the Mähler portrait—thus liberating himself from his adventure with the Akademie of December 22, 1808, an adventure that was sublime—but almost pathologically egocentric.

For all this divestment, however, Beethoven carefully preserved both the Testament and the portrait because of the insights they could communicate to posterity.

# CHAPTER SIX

## *Conclusion and Chronology*

In keeping with the elaborate vocabulary of eighteenth-century conventions for mythological and historical paintings, Mähler's 1805 portrait of Beethoven and Radoux's 1773 portrait of Beethoven's grandfather are sophisticated and richly-coded examples of the "historische Porträt."

Radoux's painting was constructed around an autobiographical plan that contains symbolic references to Beethoven's grandmother in the form of a flower-decorated band, the dilemma faced by his grandfather concerning his wife's alcoholism and the disastrous marriage that resulted, and his grandfather's resolve to rescue himself by devoting his energies to his activities as a musician.

Mähler's portrait of Beethoven—through the symbols of the fading flower of the "knotweed" plant, the uniquely-shaped lyre-guitar, the red lining of the composer's cape, his posture, and his extended right arm with uplifted hand—alludes to the composer's gradual loss of hearing (especially his inability to hear the high notes of instruments and voices), his contemplation of suicide, and his heroic rejection of that possibility.

These same subjects are ones that the composer symbolized in the "Scene by the Brook" of the *Pastoral* Scymphony, all four movements of the Symphony in C Minor, and the *Eroica*. Just as the Radoux portrayal of the composer's grandfather literally includes pages of music from Pergolesi's *La Serva padrona*, Mähler's depiction of Beethoven also symbolically references the Fourth Piano Concerto through the inclusion of the lyre-guitar (Orpheus's instrument), the temple grove and ruddy glow on the horizon (suggesting the memory of the dead and Hades), and the anthropomorphic tree (the punishing transformation of the Bacchantes into writhing oak trees).

The concerto is thus also both a "historische Porträt" and an auto-biographical narrative that relies on extensive and elaborate musical symbolic devices and references rather than visual clues or text. Its complex composition and history are retraced in the following chronology, which summarizees the artistic transformation of this most popular—and censored—myth from the Calzabigi/Gluck *Orfeo ed Euridice* of 1762 to the musical and poetic interpretations of the middle movement of Beethoven's Fourth Piano Concerto by Fanny Mendelssohn, Carl Czerny, A. B. Marx, and Franz Liszt.

## A Chronology of Beethoven's Fourth Piano Concerto

**1762**  The Calzabigi-Gluck *Orfeo ed Euridice* is premiered in Vienna; in the following three decades it becomes the most widely admired, most frequently performed, and most influential opera in Europe.

**1785**  The Calzabigi-Gluck *Orfeo ed Euridice* is performed in Bonn. The prodigiously talented Beethoven—only fourteen years old—was very likely involved as a harpsichordist.

**1785**  A German translation of Calzabigi's libretto is published in Cramer's *Magazin der Musik*. (Beethoven's mentor in Bonn was Christian Gottlob Neefe, who not only subscribed to the *Magazin der Musik* but was an occasional contributor.) Neefe doubtless shared his copies of this important journal with his student Beethoven.

**1786**  The libretto of the Biehl-Naumann *Orpheus und Euridice* (premiered in Copenhagen in January of that year) is published in the *Magazin der Musik*. Editor Cramer's introduction includes German translations of portions of both the Virgil and Ovid versions of the Orpheus legend along with a fascinating discussion of the problems involved in translating the Orpheus legend into an opera.

**1787**  The piano-vocal score of the Biehl-Naumann *Orpheus und Euridice* is published. Neefe was a subscriber to this edition, and would have shared this score with his teenage opera-loving student. (Also among the subscribers to this edition was Antonio Salieri in Vienna, to whom Beethoven later turned for instruction in the composition of recitative in opera. At some point Beethoven acquired a copy of this score; his copy was most likely a gift from Salieri, ca. 1803.)

**1787**  The Elector Max Franz sends Beethoven to Vienna to study with Mozart, but the young composer has to leave Vienna before Dittersdorf's *Die Liebe im Narrenhause,* a parody of Mozart's very successful *Die Entführung aus dem Serail,* opens to popular aclaim. In this parody the figure of Belmonte in the Mozart *Singspiel* is turned into a character named Orpheus—who pretends to be mute but expresses his emotions by playing his violin.

**1791**  The elaborately illustrated three-volume Gesellschaft edition of Ovid's *Metamorphoses* in German translation is published in Vienna. Many of Beethoven's friends and associates are sub-scribers to this important edition. Five of the illustrations in this publication would inspire graphic events in the three movements of Beethoven's concerto.

**1791**  Haydn composed *L'anima del filosofo, ossia Orfeo ed Euridice* (Lon-don). Even as this opera was in rehearsal, the production was abruptly cancelled, doubtless on the insistence of the English censors. It is possible that Haydn discussed this problem of censorship with Beethoven, since in this opera Orpheus is revealed to be a misogynist. (The misogynistic Orpheus would become an important subtext of Beethoven's "Orpheus" Concerto.)

**1800**  A six-volume edition of the complete works of Virgil in German translation is published in Vienna, the first edition of Virgil to appear in that city.

**1803**  Late August. Beethoven receives from the Parisian instrument maker Érard the gift of an innovative five-and-a-half-octave fortepiano. This instrument was triple-strung from top to bot-tom, and featured an *una corda, due corde, tre corde* pedal that was an invitation to musical dialogue—such as would occur in the second movement of the Fourth Piano Concerto.

**1803**  Early autumn. Beethoven is introduced to the amateur portrait painter Willibrord Josef Mähler.

**1804**  Beethoven produces his vast sketches for the *Eroica* Symphony. In this sketchbook are germinal thoughts for the *Pastoral* Sympho-ny, the Fourth Piano Concerto, and the Symphony in C Minor—in that sequence.

**1804**  The Friskin *bifolium* (the only other known sketch for the Fourth Piano Concerto). This brief document features a verbal reference to the lengthy dramatic trill in the second movement—that crucial moment in which Orpheus breaks his vow.

**1804** Early December. Beethoven is introduced to Friedrich August Kanne. Beethoven performs for Kanne his dialogue between Orpheus and the Furies of Hades on his new Érard fortepiano. (N.B., this is speculation.)

**1805?** Mähler paints a narrative portrait of Beethoven that contains an array of ingenious references to four major compositions. The first of these is the recently completed *Eroica* Symphony. The other works were only in the initial stages of conception. Two of these future works were the *Pastoral* Symphony and the Symphony in C Minor. The other future work—and the first to be completed—was the Fourth Piano Concerto; and in Mähler's portrait there are references to all three movements of this concerto, references having to do with the three standard chapters of the Orpheus legend: the Song of Orpheus, Orpheus in Hades, and Orpheus and the Bacchantes.

**1806** Beethoven scores his "Orpheus in Hades" as a dialogue for strings and keyboard, and then composes first and third movements of a concerto, the enframing movements of which would similarly be inspired by the Orpheus legend.

**1807** March. Beethoven's Fourth Piano Concerto is performed in a private concert at the Palais Lobkowitz.

**1807** November. *Orpheus, eine große Oper in zwei Aufzügen,* a work by Beethoven's close friend Kanne, is performed at the Court Theater in Vienna (one of the directors of which was Prince Lobkowitz). The text of the finale of this opera's first act is based line-by-line on the dialogue encountered in mm. 1-38 of the second movement of Beethoven's concerto—the "Orpheus in Hades" movement.

**1808** August. The first edition of the solo piano and orchestral parts of the Fourth Piano Concerto is published in Vienna.

**1808** December 22. Beethoven's Fourth Piano Concerto is given its first public performance in an amazing concert that had been four years in the planning. In this concert the Fourth Piano Concerto is preceded by the *Pastoral* Symphony (which the composer calls his 5th Symphony), and followed by his Symphony in C Minor (which the composer calls his 6th Symphony).

**1809?**  Following this performance of the Fourth Piano Concerto, Beethoven records an array of new thoughts that had come to him in the context of that experience. The most arresting of these new thoughts involve intensifications of specific events in Ovid's Orpheus narrative.

**1840**  In Rome Fanny Mendelssohn introduces a salon concert with the *Andante con moto* of Beethoven's Fourth Piano Concerto performed as a composition for solo piano (as a statement of "The Power of Song").

**1846**  Carl Czerny publishes his *On the Proper Performance of All Beethoven's Works for the Fortepiano,* and lists the Fourth Piano Concerto among the works he had studied with the composer. Says Czerny, " ... the entire concerto belongs to the finest and most poetical of Beethoven's creations ..." He compares the second movement to "an antique tragic scene," and explains that "The mysterious opening of the 3rd movement stands in a certain connection with the foregoing in order to complete the picturesque design."

**1859**  Adolph Bernard Marx describes in detail the debt of the *Andante con moto* of Beethoven's Fourth Piano Concerto to the Infernal Scene in the Calzabigi-Gluck *Orfeo ed Euridice.*

**1872**  Franz Liszt introduces a salon concert with the *Andante con moto* of the Fourth Piano Concerto performed as a composition for solo piano (as a statement of "The Power of Song").

Marx's 1859 identification of the *Andante con moto* of the Fourth Piano Concerto as a depiction of the "Infernal Scene" of Gluck's *Orfeo ed Euridice* answered our question of which "antique tragic scene" Czerny had alluded to in 1846. Czerny—Beethoven's pupil—had also explicitly connected the *outer* movements to the work's narrative "design. " Beethoven's own interest in cyclic organization across entire works, which came to a peak in a group of important compositions written during the years 1804-08, helps support Czerny's assertion that all of the movements are unified by a single "idea." Whereas the finale of the *Eroica* has been shown to be the generative movement of that symphony, as convincingly demonstrated by Lewis Lockwood, so the movement that  later fascinated Fanny Mendelssohn, Marx, and Liszt—"Orpheus in Hades"—generated the outer movements of the concerto.

As we have seen, in the middle movement Beethoven's approach to the Classical accounts of the Orpheus legend was to compose an event-by-event musical narrative. In the first and third movements—"The Song of Orpheus" and "Orpheus and the Bacchantes"—Beethoven worked quite differently. In these two chapters on Ovid's text, one rarely encounters passages that invite or permit narrative treatment in music. What is more important, the elaborate conventions of the first and last movements of the Classical concerto forbade such an approach.

In the opening pages of the first and third movements Beethoven presents a sequence of musical ideas reflecting a sequence of thoughts that occur at the outset of these two episodes in Ovid's narrative. Important subordinate themes reflect important subsequent events in Ovid's stories. The developmental sections of both movements are based on the central conflicts in the stories found in these two chapters of the Orpheus legend. Finally, the closing pages of the outer movements bring each chapter to its appropriate conclusion. At the end of the first movement, Beethoven lingers on the three most important concerns of "The Song of Orpheus." At the finale's end he creates an elaborate string of events that provide a dénouement not only for that movement but for the whole adventure with the Orpheus legend. Of all Beethoven's music, the Fourth Piano Concerto is his most intensely poetic invention because it is so densely and consistently inspired by poetic imagery.

The process of transformation that is one of the central themes of Ovid's *Metamorphoses* became the governing process of the Fourth Piano Concerto in a great variety of ingenious musical ways. Beethoven's most elaborate application of transformation appears in the many different uses of the A theme of the finale. As the movement progresses, we discover that, although Orpheus is destroyed by the Bacchantes, his lyre is rescued and transfigured as a statement of the triumph of virtue over wickedness. Indeed, over the course of the entire concerto, an Ovidian morality play unfolds in which victory is ultimately granted to the lyre, the symbol of music itself. As the lyre comes to represent Orpheus' companion protagonist, music itself became Beethoven's companion protagonist in the years following the Heiligenstadt Testament:

> I would have ended my life—it was only my art that held me back. Ah, it seemed impossible to leave this world until I had brought forth all that I felt was within me.

That resolution—that victory would ultimately be granted to music—became richly symbolized in the narrative of one of his "finest and most poetical creations," the Fourth Piano Concerto.

# APPENDIX A

## Discography of Recordings of Beethoven's Fourth Piano Concerto Performed on Period Instruments

At the time of the publication of this book eight recordings of Beethoven's Fourth Piano Concerto in performances using period instruments had been released.

1. **1972.** Harmonia Mundi 065-99 657. Collegium Aureum (Vienna). Franzjosef Maier, concertmaster. Paul Badura-Skoda, fortepianist. 6 ½-octave fortepiano by Conrad Graf, ca. 1820. Program notes by Paul Badura-Skoda, Duration of the *Andante con moto*, 4'42". ℗ 1972. Reissued (1) as an LP by BASF KBH 21510 in 1973 with program notes in English, French and German, © 1973; (2) as an LP by Harmonia Mundi (BAC 3002) in 1974 with program notes in English and French, ℗ 1974, © 1974; and (3) as a compact disc with the Triple Concerto in 1988: Deutsche Harmonia Mundi 77063-2-RG (Badura-Skoda's notes on this reissue are much abbreviated and do not contain information on Czerny and Orpheus or details on the importance of performance on period instruments). ℗ 1972, 1988, © 1990.

Ths is the first recording ever published of any Beethoven concerto performed on original instruments. In his notes for the 1972 issue, Badura-Skoda cites the traditional view that the *Andante con moto* was inspired by the legendary scene of Orpheus in Hades:

> After the light first movement which employs the high register of the piano as never before, the tragic dark *Andante con moto* introduces an extreme contrast. Following a tradition passed on by word of mouth, this movement was inspred by a classical scene. The relentless 'no' of the Gods at the beginning is gradually softened by the cries of Orpheus, whose song soars into the highest spheres, but then, after the disappearance of the beloved shadow, descends into an outbreak of despair [solo cadenza]—even the Gods are moved.

(This is the English translation from the 1973 re-release of the 1972 French original.)

2. **1988.** L'Oiseau-Lyre 421 408-2. Academy of Ancient Music (London),
   Christopher Hogwood, conductor. Steven Lubin, fortepianist. (With
   Concertos nos. 1, 2, 3, 5.) 6 ½-octave fortepiano by Rodney J.
   Regier (1980), a copy of an instrument by Conrad Graf (Vienna,
   1824). Program notes, "Beethoven's 'Orpheus' Concerto" by Owen
   Jander. Additional program notes by Robert Winter ("Beethoven
   and the Piano Concerto") and Steven Lubin ("Beethoven's
   Pianos"). Opus 58 recorded in August-September 1987.
   Duration of the *Andante con moto*: 4'34". ℗ 1988, © 1988.
   Re-released with the addition of sonatas recorded in 1989 by
   Decca in 2006. 475 7297 (475 7298-475 7300).

Lubin and Hogwood observe Czerny's instructions for the performance
of the second movement: "It must not be played too slow, though the
pianist may restrain the time rather more than the Orchestra." Here we
first encounter this playoff of two tempi. The movement indeed projects
as "an antique tragic scene." The recordings by Newman and Immerseel
below also feature these essential contrasts of tempo between the soloist
and the orchestra. My notes, which argue that all three movements are
related to Orpheus, contain an abbreviated early version of the material
in this book.

3. **1988.** Newport Classic, NCD 60081. Philomusica Antiqua (New York),
   Stephen Simon, conductor. Anthony Newman, fortepianist.
   (With Concerto no. 2.) Fortepiano a copy of an 1804 English
   grand built by Robert Smith of Boston. Program notes with
   analytical index by Anthony Lewis. Duration of the *Andante con
   moto* 4'33". ℗ 1988, © 1988. Re-released in *BBC Music Magazine*
   ("winter special 1995") on a CD with works by Corelli, Vivaldi,
   and Bach.

Lewis "plays the continuo part on the fortepiano during the orchestra-only
sections." "Tempos (in beats per minute) as recommended by Czerny, or
from the collated Beethoven tempos by Rudolf Kolisch, *Musical Quarterly*,
1943." In his notes Newman observes:

> With the Fourth Concerto we enter into a new world of concerto writing, a
> kind of fantasy concerto which incorporates traditional form with a com-
> pletely different way of viewing the concerto format [pp. 2-3].

4. **1989.** EMI CDC 7 498152. The London Classical Players, Roger
   Norrington, conductor, Melvyn Tan, fortepianist. 6-octave fortepiano by Derek Adlam (1983), a copy of an instrument by
   Nanette Streicher (Vienna, 1814). Program notes by Douglas
   Johnson with "performance note" from Roger Norrington and
   "note on Melvyn Tan's fortepiano" by Derek Adlam. Recorded
   in July 1988. Duration of the *Andante con moto* 4"06". ℗ 1989.
   Re-released with the set of complete concertos by Virgin Classics
   in 2008.

The fortepiano used for this recording has an *una corda* pedal, bassoon
pedal, moderator, and sustain pedal. In his notes, Johnson writes:

> All three movements flout convention: the first with its hushed opening
> G-major phrase in the piano answered by an apparently disbelieving orchestra
> in B Major; the last with its cheeky pretence at C Major, at once nonchalent
> and yet subtly implied (or so it seems) by events in the first two movements.
> And of course the *Andante [con moto]*, its gruff string recitatives and cantabile
> solo phrases testing the power of poetry to tame harsh reality. Whether the
> inspiration was Gluck's *Orfeo*, as some have thought, or something deeper
> in Beethoven consciousness, this movement has remained beyond imitation
> [pp. 3-4].

5. **1997.** Sony SK62684. Tafelmusik (Toronto). Bruno Weil,conductor. Jos
   van Immerseel, fortepianist. (With Concerto no. 3.) Fortepiano by
   Johann Neomuk Tröndlin (Leipzig), ca. 1810, restored by Jan ven
   den Hemel (Antwerp) in 1996. Six octaves plus two notes. Program notes by H.C. Robbins Landon (regarding the concertos)
   and Jos van Immerseel (on the fortepiano). Recorded September
   1996. Duration of the *Andante con moto*: 3'55". ℗ 1997, © 1997.

The contrast of tempos and characteriztions of Orpheus' and the Furies'
music here is arrestingly dramatic. Even with the subtle slowing of tempo
in the piano sections, this performance is the shortest of all eight (and a full
1'29" shorter than Levin's recording below!) The fortepiano from 1810 is
particularly beautiful. According to Robbin Landon's notes:

> For many people this is the most perfect, the most personal, most tender of
> all Beethoven's piano concertos. Like Mozart's K. 271, the piano opens the
> work all by itself and the orchestra reveals itself coyly, like a young maiden,
> until we realize that it is indeed a grand orchestra, even to trumpets and
> drums, which, dramatically, do not enter until the finale. The rhapsodic
> slow movement is in the great tradition of an instrument pretending to be a
> human voice—the *recitativo accompagnato* that was to figure so effectively in
> the Ninth Symphony's Finale [p. 9].

6. 1998. Archiv Produktion 289 457 608-2. Orchestre Révolutionnaire et Romantique. John Eliot Gardner, conductor. Robert Levin, forte-pianist. (With Concertos nos. 1, 2, 3, 5; Rondo, WoO 6; and the Choral Fantasy.) Copy of a Walter & Sohn fortepiano (c. 1805) by Paul McNulty (Prague, 1997) from the collection of Harvard University. Program notes, ""Beethoven: The Five Piano Concertos, Rondo, WoO6, Choral Fantasy," by Robert Levin. Recorded in November, 1997. Duration of the *Andante con moto*: 5'24". ℗ 1998. Reissued in the set: Archiv Produktion 459-622-2.

"All lead-ins and cadenzas improvised by Robert Levin." In his notes on the Fourth Concerto, Levin writes:

> The Fourth Concerto is perhaps the most sublime work of this period, and hence of the entire concerto literature. Its second movement, stripped of abstract form to speak in an unbroken arc of poignancy and calamity, quickly became associated with Orpheus and the Furies. Owen Jander has made a persuasive case that the music follows the text of a vernacular version of the legend being acted out on the street corners of Vienna at the time of the concerto's gestation. In keeping with the personification of Orpheus and his lyre, I have introduced a substantial amount of arpeggiation into the chordal accompaniment. The movement calls for a piano capable of true *una corda*—that is, with a lever that shifts the hammers from striking all three strings to two or only one. ... Beethoven prescribes *una corda* except at the movement's climax, where he requires a shift to two and then three strings as part of the crescendo from *pianissimo* to *fortissimo*, reverting to two and then one string in the return to *pianissimo*. The dynamic range of this passage when executed on an instrument conforming to Beethoven's requirements—as in the present recording—is utterly terrifing. Whether one wishes to apply Jander's analogy to the outer movements (he terms the first "The Song of Orpheus" and the last "Orpheus and the Bacchantes"), thereby addressing the withholding of the trumpets and drums until the finale, there is little question that the first movement changes the possibilities of the concerto forever [pp. 11-12].

7. **1999**. Archiv Producktion 474 224-2. Version for piano and string quintet in the reconstruction of Hans-Werner Küthen(1996). (With the chamber version of Symphony no. 2.) Members of the Orchestre Révolutionnaire et Romantique with Robert Levin, fortepianist (fortepiano not identified). Program notes by Ingo Harden. Recorded in December 1997. Duration of the *Andante con moto*: 5'14". ℗ 1999, © 2003.

"Lead-ins and cadenzas improvised by Robert Levin."

8. **2005**. Alpha Productions 079. Ensemble Cristofori. Arthur Schoonderwörd, fortepianist. (With Concerto no. 5.) Johann Fritz fortepiano
from 1807-1810. Program notes by Denis Grenier (on Jacques
Louis David's "Portrait of Pierre Sériziat," 1795) and Schoonderwörd ("Vienna under the Spell of Napoleon," "Érard's Influence
on Viennese Piano Making," "Beethoven and Archduke Rudolph,"
"Beethoven's Fourth Piano Concerto," "Beethoven's Fifth Piano
Concerto," "Performance Practice Research," and "The Piano-
forte"). Recorded September 2004. Duration of the *Andante con
moto*: 3'56". ℗ 2004, © 2005.

The fortepiano used for this recording "is one of the earliest known
Viennese six-octave instruments with an una corda stop." The compass of
the instrument is FF to f4; the other three pedals are linked bassoon and
moderator pedal, moderator, and dampers. The orchestra is unique among
this set of recordings because the make-up of the orchestra mimics the
forces that performed the work in Prince Lobkowitz's palace. According to
Schoonderwörd's notes:

> In the light of these facts [in Stefan Weinzierl's exceptional book *Beethovens
> Konzerträume Raumakustik und symphonische Aufführungspraxis an der Schwelle
> zum modernen Konzertwesen* (Beethoven's Concert Spaces, Room-Acoustics,
> and Symphonic Performance Practices at the Threshold of Modern Concert
> Practices), published in 2002] and Beethoven's directions in the manuscripts
> of the fourth and fifth piano concertos, I decided to opt for a logical and
> well-balanced orchestra as it may have sounded in Lobkowitz's palace. With
> the exception of the flute, the fourth concerto has the same instrumentation
> as the fifth, and the complete orchestra for the present recording therefore
> comprised 20 and 21 persons respectively [p. 31].

Schoonderwörd theorizes that Schiller's 1796 poem "Der neue Orpheus"
(published in *Die Horen*) "may well have been the source of Beethoven's
inspiration for the first movement of his Fourth Piano Concerto." (The
poem, included in the original German in the notes without English
translation, remakes the love story between Orpheus and "Chloe.")

> Orpheus, the poet and musician, takes his place at the piano to express his
> love for Chloe and to attempt to win her heart with flattery, requests and
> sighs, melting chords and soft harmonies. The musicologist Owen Jander has
> argued that the second movement is set in the underworld, where Orpheus
> tries to save his lost love from the hands of Hades and the Furies.  With
> his poetry, love, and beautiful playing, he finally succeeds—and Beethoven
> prescribes the una corda stop—until ... The final movement depicts the
> euphoria of Orpheus' return to the world above with his love and with the
> joy of the crowd the work comes to an end in pastoral surroundings [p. 29].

# APPENDIX B

## *The Missing Sketchbook*

It is a matter of profound regret to all musicians, musicologists, and music lovers who are fascinated by Beethoven's Fourth Piano Concerto that the composer's sketchbook for this work is missing. On a speculative basis I present five possible explanations.

**Speculation 1.** This sketchbook, though missing, still exists—in someone's attic, perhaps? This, of course, is what we all hope will be the case—and that the sketchbook for Beethoven's op. 58 will eventually come to light. What clues will it provide to Beethoven Orphic plan?

One recalls the situation with Beethoven's early string quartet, op. 18, no. 1, where the sketches for the coda of the slow movement are fitted with remarks in French that have to do with the crypt scene in Daniel Steibelt's *Romeo et Juliette.* Very likely Beethoven's sketches for his Fourth Piano Concerto will include similar remarks having to do with the Orpheus legend. What a fascinating sketchbook that will be!

**Speculation 2.** Alas, it seems more likely that the sketchbook for Beethoven's op. 58 is missing because it was destroyed. Accidentally destroyed by fire, perhaps. Who knows?

**Speculation 3.** Perhaps this precious sketchbook was accidentally destroyed by some unwitting fool who had no awareness of the enormous importance of all those pages, cluttered with such a bewildering array of strange scratchings.

But how, we ask, could that sketchbook have found its way into the hands of such an unwitting fool?

**Speculation 4.** The next possibility is that the sketchbook for Beethoven's Fourth Piano Concerto was purposefully destroyed. Hard as it is to imagine, it must be granted that Beethoven himself could have destroyed the sketchbook for his opus 58. But why would Beethoven—normally so protective of his sketchbooks—have done such a thing?

One recalls the footnote in Czerny's *On the Proper Performance* reporting that Beethoven was aware that there are many people who prefer to listen to music without having their imaginations "fettered" by a definitely-expressed object. But would Beethoven have destroyed the sketchbook of his "Orpheus" Concerto out of concern for such narrow-minded music lovers?

**Speculation 5.** The most likely possibility is that Beethoven's sketchbook for his "Orpheus" Concerto was destroyed by his strange friend, Anton Schindler. It is known that just after Beethoven died, Schindler carried off all of the composer's conversation books—reportedly some 400 of these. Many years later Schindler sold his trove of Beethoven's conversation books to the Royal Library in Berlin. In Schindler's "trove," however, there were now only 136 conversation books.

In those 136 conversation books, scholars have detected a great many fraudulent entries in Schindler's hand. Schindler was planning to write a biography of Beethoven; and the purpose of these fraudulent entries was to lead future scholars to believe that Schindler was a frequent participant in conversations between Beethoven and his various friends—which turns out not to have been the case anywhere near as often as Shindler would have had us believe.

With the awareness of this pattern of deceptive behavior, what, we ask, had this Beethoven biographer found in those missing 264 books that caused him to destroy them? What was Schindler out to erase?

During the many years when Beethoven was losing his hearing he always remained in touch with Friedrich August Kanne, that "Du Freund" whom he had met back in 1804. These two middle-age bachelors often dined together; and on those occasions whatever Kanne wanted to communicate to his "Du Freund" Beethoven, he would of course have written in those conversation books. In the 136 surviving conversation books, however, the handwriting of Kanne is infrequently encountered. Ergo, one of Schindler's goals—perhaps his principal goal—was to extract the many communications between Beethoven and Kanne. I suspect that in those conversation books that Schindler destroyed were various discussions that touched on the subject of homosexuality. History, Schindler decided, should be shielded from any such awareness.

I finally speculate that it was Schindler who destroyed the sketchbook for Beethoven's Fourth Piano Concerto—and for the same reason. The many folios in this volume would have contained a consistent flow of texted musical ideas that revealed this concerto's involvement with the figure of Orpheus, "the author of Greek love." History, Schindler again decided, should above all be shielded from that awareness.

# BIBLIOGRAPHY

## PRIMARY SOURCES

Breuning, Gerhard von. *Memories of Beethoven from the House of the Black-Robed Spaniards.* Edited by Maynard Solomon. Translated by Henry F. Mins and Maynard Solomon. Cambridge: Cambridge University Press, 1992. Originally published as *Aus dem Schwarzspanierhause* (Vienna: Rosner, 1874).

Schindler, Anton. *Beethoven As I Knew Him*, 3rd ed. Edited by Donald MacArdle. Translated by Constance S. Jolly. Chapel Hill: North Carolina University Press, 1966. Translation of *Biographie von Ludwig van Beethoven*, 3rd ed. (Münster: Aschendorff, 1860).

Wegeler, Franz Gerhard, and Ferdinand Ries. *Beethoven Remembered: The Biographical Notes of Franz Wegeler and Ferdinand Ries.* Translated and edited by Frederick Noonan. Arlington, Virginia: Great Ocean Publishers, 1987. Originally published as *Biographische Notizen überLudwig van Beethoven.* (Coblenz: K. Badeker, 1838).

## BOOKS AND SCORES IN BEETHOVEN'S LIBRARY

Bode, Johann Elert. *Anleitung zur Kenntnis des gestirnten Himmels mit Kupfern.* 7th ed. Berlin: C. F. Himburg, 1801. (For information on Beethoven's library, see Albert Leitzmann, *Ludwig van Beethoven*, 2 vols., Leipzig: Insel-Verlag, 1921, 2:379-83 [this item is in the second list, no. 34], and Thayer-Forbes, 1061-70.)

Naumann, Johann Gottlieb. *Orpheus und Euridice.* Kiel: C. F. Cramer, 1787. (See Thayer-Forbes, 1061.)

Sturm, Christoph. *Betrachtungen über die Werke Gottes im Reiche der Natur und der Vorsehung auf alle Tages des Jahres.* 3rd ed. 2 vols. Reutlingen: [publisher not identified], 1811. (See Leitzmann, no. 4. Beethoven's copy is in the Deutsche Staatsbibliothek, Berlin, autograph 40.2.)

## LETTERS

Albrecht, Theodore, trans. and ed. *Letters to Beethoven and Other Correspondence.* 3 vols. Lincoln: Nebraska University Press, 1996.

Anderson, Emily, trans. and ed. *The Letters of Beethoven.* 3 vols. London: Macmillan, 1961. Reprint, New York: Norton, 1985.

Brandenburg, Sieghard, ed. *Ludwig van Beethoven, Briefwechsel Gesamtausgabe.* 7 vols. Munich: G. Henle Verlag, 1996-98.


## SKETCHBOOK STUDIES

Frohlich, Martha. "Sketches for Beethoven's Fourth and Fifth: a Long-Neglected Source." *Bonner Beethoven-Studien* 1 (1999): 29-48.

Johnson, Douglas, Alan Tyson, and Robert Winter. *The Beethoven Sketchbooks: History, Reconstruction, Inventory.* Berkeley: University of California Press, 1985.

Nottenbohm, Gustav. *Zwei Skizzenbücher von Beethoven aus dem Jahren 1801 bis 1803.* Forward by Paul Mies. Leipzig: Breitkopf & Härtel, 1924. Reprint, Wiesbaden: Dr. Martin Sändig, 1970. (Includes "Ein Skizzenbuch von Beethoven," originally published in 1865, and "Ein Skizzenbuch von Beethoven aus dem Jahre 1803," originally published in 1880.)

Wade, Rachel. "Beethoven's *Eroica* Sketchbook." *Fontes Artis Musicae* 24 (1977): 25-89.


## EARLY TREATISES AND PERIODICALS

Cramer, Carl Friedrich, ed. *Magazin der Musik.* 4 vols. Hamburg: Musikalischen Niederlage, 1783-86. Facsimile, Hildesheim: G. Olms, 1971.

Czerny, Carl. *Über den richtigen Vortrag der sämtlichen Beethoven'schen Klavierwerke.* Vienna: A. Diabelli u. Comp., [1842]. Facsimile edited by Paul Badura-Skoda, Vienna: Universal Edition, 1963. Contemporaneous English translation: *On the Proper Performance of All Beethoven's Works for the Piano.* London: R. Cocks & Co., n.d. Facsimile edition by Paul Badura-Skoda, Vienna: Universal Edition, 1970.

Engel, Johann Jakob. *Ideen zu einer Mimik.* 2 vols. Berlin: J. J. Engel. 1785-86.

Koch, Heinrich Christoph. *Versuch einer Anleitung zur Composition*. 3 vols.
    Leipzig: Böhm, 1782, 1787, 1793. English version of sections 3 and
    4 translated with introduction by Nancy Kovaleff Baker. *Introduc-
    tory Essay on Composition: The Mechanical Rules of Melody*.
    New Haven: Yale University Press, 1983.

Rochlitz, Friedrich, ed. *Allgemeine musikalische Zeitung*. Leipzig: Breitkopf
    & Härtel, 1798-1848, 1863-68.

Sulzer, Johann Georg. *Allgemeine Theorie der schönen Künste*. 2 vols.
    Leipzig: M. G. Weidemann, 1771 and 1774. Reprint, Leipzig:
    M. G. Weidemann, 1774. 2nd ed. Leipzig: M. G. Weidemann, 1778
    and 1779. 3rd ed. with bibliographies by Friedrich von Blanken-
    burg, 4 vols. Leipzig: M. G. Weidemann, 1792-94; index 1799.
    Facsimile, Hildesheim: G. Olms, 1970.


**EARLY SCORES**

Bach, C. P. E. *Magnificat*. 1794. Bonn: Nikolaus Simrock, n.d.

Bach, Johann Sebastian. *Magnificat*. ca. 1728-31.


**CLASSICAL TEXTS (EDITIONS THAT EXISTED IN BEETHOVEN'S DAY)**

Hyginus, Gaius Julius. *Poeticon Astronomicon*. Lyons: Lugduni Batavorum,
    1742.

*Les Métamophoses d'Ovide, en latin et en français, de la traduction de M. l'abbé
    Banier* ... 4 vols. 140 engraved illustrations. Paris: 1767-70. This
    sumptuous edition was financed by a consortium of publishers in
    Paris (including Delalain, Delormel, Despilly, Guillyn, Hochereau,
    Le Mire et Bassans, Panckoucke, Pissot, and Prault), each of whom
    sold these volumes with his own title pages.

*Les Métamophoses d'Ovide gravées sur les desseins des meilleurs peintres fran-
    çais*. Paris: Le Mire et Bassans, 1771. This was a limited edition of
    the first copies of the engraved illustrations for the above
    publication.

*Ovids Verwandlungen, in Kupfern vorgestellt*. 3 vols. Vienna: Herausgegeben
    von einer Gesellschaft, 1791. This edition features 140 engraved
    illustrations copied from the Parisian edition of 1767-79. It also
    reports the names of more than 650 subscribers, about a dozen of
    whom were friends of Beethoven.

*Ovids Verwandlungen travestiert von Gottlieb Müller*. Books 10 and 11.
     Vienna: Peter Rehm's sel. Witwe, 1807. This was from a series of
     fourteen pocket-size volumes published between 1804 and 1807,
     each volume dealing with a single book of Ovid's Metamorphoses
     (which is in fifteen books). In this series, Books 10 and 11 were
     published in a single volume since these contain the story of Or-
     pheus.

*P. Virgilius Maro sämmtliche Werke*. Translated Johann Heinrich Voss. 6
     vols. Vienna: Joseph Dehler, 1800-01.

## OPERAS

Benda, Friedrich. *Orpheus, ein Singspiel in drey Aufzügen*. Libretto by
     Gottfried Ferdinand von Lindemann. Berlin: 1785. Piano-vocal
     score, Berlin: Rellstab, 1787.

Benda, Georg. *Romeo und Julie*. Libretto by Friedrich Willhelm Gotter.
     Gotha: 1776, Bonn: 1782.

Dittersdorf, Karl Ditters von. *Die Liebe im Narrenhause*. Libretto by
     Gottlieb Stephanie der Jüngere. Vienna: 1787.

Gluck, Christoph Willibald. *Orfeo ed Euridice*. Libretto by Ranieri
     Calzabigi. Vienna: 1762, Bonn: 1785.

Haydn, Franz Joseph. *L'anima del filosofo, ossia Orfeo ed Euridice*. Libretto
     by Carlo Francesco Badini. London: 1791 (but not performed
     in Haydn's lifetime).

Kanne, August Friedrich (composer and librettist). *Orpheus, eine grosse
     Oper in zwey Aufzügen*. Vienna: 1807.

Naumann, Johann Gottlieb. *Orpheus og Euridice*. Libretto by Charlotte
     Dorothea Biehl. Copenhagen: 1786. Libretto in Cramer's
     Magazin der Musik 2, no. 2 (1786): 1085-1145. Piano-vocal score
     titled *Orpheus und Euridice*. Kiel: C. F. Cramer, 1787.

Pergolesi, Giovanni. *La serva padrona*. Libretto by Gennaro Antonio Fed-
     erico. Naples: 1733, Bonn: sometime in the 1760s.

Steibelt, Daniel. *Roméo et Juliette*. Libretto by J. A. P. de Ségur. Paris: 1793.
     Orchestral score, Paris: Boyer, [1793].

Zingarelli, Antonio, and Girolamo Crescentini. *Giulietta e Romeo*. Libretto
     by Giuseppe Maria Foppa. Milan: 1796, Vienna: 1797 (revival, 1804).
     The music for Romeo was composed by the castrato Girolamo Cres-
     centini, who sang the role in the productions in Milan and Vienna.

## STUDIES OF MUSICAL INSTRUMENTS

Bonner, Stephen. *The Classical Image: European History and Manufacture of the Lyre Guitar, 858-1848.* Harlow: Bois de Boulogne, 1972.

"Einige Worte über die neue französische Lyra (Lyre-Guitarre)." *Allgemeine musikalische Zeitung* 3, no. 47 (August 19, 1801): 786-89. The author is anonymous.

Luithlen, Victor. *Katalog der Sammlung alter Musikinstrumente: 1. Teil, Saiteninstrumente.* Vienna: Kunsthistorisches Museum, 1966.

## STUDIES OF PAINTINGS AND RELATED SUBJECTS

Berckenhagen, Ekhart. *Anton Graff: Leben und Werke.* Berlin: Deutsche Verlag für Kunstwissenschaft, 1967.

Börsch-Supan, Helmut. *Caspar David Friedrich.* Translated by Sarah Twohig and John William Gabriel. Munich: Prestel-Verlag, 1990.

*Caspar David Friedrich: Das gesamte graphische Werk.* Herrsching: Manfred Pawlak, n.d.

Colton, Judith. "From Voltaire to Buffon: Further Observations on Nudity, Heroic and Otherwise." In *Art, the Ape of Nature: Studies in Honor of H. W. Janson,* edited by Moshe Barasch and Lucy Freeman Sandler, 531-48. New York: H. N. Abrams, 1981.

Connelly, James L. "The Grand Gallery of the Louvre and the Museum Project." *Journal of the Society of Architectural Historians* 31, no. 1 (March 1972): 120-37.

Everett, Thomas H. "Polyganum bistorta." *The New York Botanical Garden Illustrated Encyclopedia of Horticulture.* 10 vols. New York: Garland Publishers, 1982. Vol. 8:2749.

Gaborit, Jean-René. *Jean-Baptiste Pigalle, 1714-1785: Sculptures de Musée du Louvre.* Paris: Editions de la Réunion des musées nationaux, 1985.

Glück, Franz. "W. J. Mählers Beethovenbildnisse und seiner Porträte anderer Persönlichkeiten." *Alte und modern Kunste* 6, no. 45 (1961): 11-16.

Jander, Owen. "'Let Your Deafness No Longer be a Secret—Even in Art': Self-Portraiture and the Third Movement of the C Minor Symphony." *Beethoven Forum* 8 (2000): 25-70.

____. "The Prophetic Conversation in Beethoven's 'Scene by the Brook.'" *The Musical Quarterly* 77, no. 3 (Fall 1993): 508-59.

____. "The Radoux Portrait of Beethoven's Grandfather; its Symbolic Meaning." *Imago Musicae* 6 (1989): 83-107.

Koerner, Joseph Leo. *Caspar David Friedrich and the Subject of Landscape.* New Haven and London: Yale University Press, 1990.

McClellan, Andrew L. "The Politics and Aesthetics of Display: Museums in Paris 1750-1800." *Art History* 7 (1984): 438-64.

Oppenheimer, Margaret A. "Nisa Villers, née Lemoine (1774-1821)." *Gazette des Beaux-Arts* ser. 6, v. 127 (April 1996): 165-80.

Robbins Landon, H. C., comp. and ed. *Beethoven: a Documentary Study.* New York: Macmillan, 1970.

Schmied, Wieland. *Friedrich.* Translated by Russell Stockman. New York: Harry N. Abrams, 1995.

Seznec, Jean, and Jean Adhémar. *Diderot Salons.* 4 vols. Oxford: Clarendon Press, 1957-67.

Van der Zanden, Jos. "'Out of Love, or Out of Pity?': A Musical Message from Louis van Beethoven." *The Beethoven Journal* 15, no. 2 (Winter 2000): 50-56.

Vaughan, William, Helmut Börsch-Supan, and Hans Joachim Neidhardt. *Caspar David Friedrich, 1774-1840: Romantic Landscape Painting in Dresden.* London: Tate Gallery, 1972.

## 18TH- AND 19TH-CENTURY LITERATURE

Hanslick, Eduard. *Geschichte des Concertwesens in Wien.* Vienna: Wilhelm Braumüller, 1869. Reprinted, Hildesheim: Olms Verlag, 1979.

Hensel, Sebastian. *The Mendelssohn Family, 1729-1847.* 2 vols. New York: Harper & Brothers, 1882.

Krebs, Karl. *Dittersdorfiana.* Berlin: Gebrüder Paetel, 1900. Reprint, 1972.

Marx, Adolf Bernhard. *Ludwig van Beethoven: Leben und Schaffen.* 2 vols. Berlin: Otto Janke, 1859. 6th ed., 1911.

____. *Gluck und die Oper.* 2 vols. Berlin: O. Janke, 1863.

Mayer, Anton. *Wiens Buchdrucker-Geschichte, 1482-1882.* 2 vols. Vienna: W. Frick, 1883-87.

Neefe, Christian Gottlieb. "The Life of Christian Gottlieb Neefe." *Forgotten Musicians.* Translated and edited by Paul Nettl, 246-64. New York: Philosophical Library, 1951.

Reichardt, Johann Friedrich. *Vertraute Briefe geschrieben auf einer Reise nach Wien und den oesterreichischen Staaten zu Ende des Jahres 1808 und zu Anfang 1809.* Amsterdam: Kunst-u. Industrie-Comptoir, 1810. Excerpt in English translation in Oliver Strunk, *Source Readings in Music History,* 737-39. New York: Norton, 1950.

Thayer, Alexander Wheelock. *Thayer's Life of Beethoven.* Revised and edited by Elliot Forbes. 2 vols. Princeton: Princeton University Press, 1964.

## 20TH- AND 21ST-CENTURY LITERATURE

Bauman, Thomas. *North German Opera in the Age of Goethe.* Cambridge: Cambridge University Press, 1985.

Brechka, Frank T. *Gerhard van Swieten and His World, 1700-1772.* The Hague: M. Nijhoff, 1970.

Cone, Edward T. "Beethoven's Orpheus—or Jander's?" *19th-Century Music* 8 (1985): 283-86.

Cooper, Barry. "Beethoven's Revisions to His Fourth Piano Concerto." In *Performing Beethoven,* edited by Robin Stowell, 23-48. Cambridge: Cambridge University Press, 1994.

Dahlsgard, Inga. *Women in Denmark, Yesterday and Today.* Copenhagen: Det Danske Selskab, 1980.

Fellinger, Imogen. "Friedrich August Kanne als Kritiker Beethovens." In *Bericht über den internationalen musikwissenschaftlichen Kongress Bonn 1970,* edited by Carl Dahlhaus, et al., 383-86. Kassel: Bärenreiter Verlag, 1972.

Haberl, Dieter. "Beethovens erste Reise nach Wien–Die Datierung seiner Schülerreise zu W. A. Mozart." *Neues Musikwissenschaftliches Jahrbuch* 14 (2006): 215-55.

Hitzig, Wilhelm. "Aus dem Briefen Griesingers an Breitkopf & Härtel entnommene Notizen über Beethoven." *Der Bär* 4 (1927): 23-24.

Jander, Owen. "Adolph Bernhard Marx, Victim of the Post-Schering Syndrome." *The Beethoven Journal* 10, no. 1 (Spring 1995): 6-18.

_____. "Beethoven's 'Orpheus in Hades': The Andante con moto of the Fourth Piano Concerto." *19th-Century Music* 8, no. 3 (Spring 1985): 195-212.

_____. "Beethoven's Philosophical Monologue Regarding the Route to Rescue from His Fate: The Andante con moto of his Symphony in C Minor." *The Beethoven Journal* 22, no. 2 (2007): 50-86.

_____. "'Cramer, Cramer! We Shall Never Be Able To Do Anything Like That!': Understanding a Favorite Quotation about Mozart's Concerto in C Minor, K. 491, and Mozart's Influence on Beethoven's Concertos." *The Beethoven Journal* 15, no. 2 (Winter 2000): 57-63.

_____. "Exploring Sulzer's Allgemeine Theorie as a Source Used by Beethoven." *The Beethoven Newsletter* 2, no. 1 (Spring 1987): 1-7.

_____. "Genius in the Arena of Charlatanry: The First Movement of Beethoven's 'Tempest' Sonata in Cultural Context." In *Musica Franca: Essays in Honor of Frank D'Accone*, edited by Irene Alm, Alyson McLamore, and Colleen Reardon, 585-630. Stuyvesant, New York: Pendragon Press, 1996.

_____. "The 'Kreutzer' Sonata as Dialogue." *Early Music* 16, no. 1 (February 1988): 34-49.-

_____. "Orpheus Revisited: A Ten-Year Retrospect on the Andante con moto of Beethoven's Fourth Piano Concerto." *19th-Century Music* 19, no. 1 (Summer 1995): 33-49.

_____. "The Three Chapters of the Orpheus Myth as They Figure in Librettos of Operas: the Favorite Episode, the Subject Avoided, and the Theme Cultivated." In *Words on Music: Essays in Honor of Andrew Porter on the Occasion of His 75th Birthday*, edited by David Rosen and Claire Brook, 52-170. Pendragon Press, Hillsdale, New York, 2003.

Kirkendale, Warren. "New Roads to Old Ideas in Beethoven's *Missa solemnis*." *The Musical Quarterly* 56, no. 4 (October 1970): 665-701.

Kramer, Richard. "Beethoven and Carl Heinrich Graun." In *Beethoven Studies* [1], edited by Alan Tyson, 18-24. New York: Norton, 1973.

Solomon, Maynard. *Beethoven*. 2nd revised edition. New York: Norton, 1973.

Sterba, Editha and Richard. *Beethoven and His Nephew.* New York: Pantheon, 1954.

Szász, Tibor. "Beethoven's Basso Continuo: Notation and Performance." In *Performing Beethoven,* edited by Robin Stowell, 1-22. Cambridge: Cambridge University Press, 1994.

Tovey, Donald Francis. *Essays in Musical Analysis.* Vol. 3: Concertos. London: Oxford University Press, 1936.

Ulrich, Hermann. "Beethoven's Freund Friedrich August Kanne." *Oesterreichische Musikzeitung* 29 (1974): 75-80.

Wagner, Cosima. *Cosima Wagner's Diaries.* Vol. I (1868-1877). Edited by Martin Gregor-Dellin and Dietrich Mack. Translated by Geoffry Skelton. New York: Harcourt Brace Jovanoch, 1976.

Wagner, Walter. *Die Geschichte der Akademie der Bildenden Künste in Wien.* Vienna: Brüder Rosenbaum, 1967.

Witcombe, Charles C. "Beethoven's Religion. An English Translation and Analysis of the Composer's Markings in Christoph Sturm's Betrachtungen." M.A. thesis, San José State University, 1998.

# General Index

Orpheus, Euridice, and the Orpheus myth in general—being the subjects of this book—are not indexed. (See, however, pp. 40-41 and 132-34 for discussions of historical treatments of the character of Euridice in operas on the Orpheus legend.)

# Beethoven Works Index

Choral Fantasy: 193
*Fidelio*, op. 72: 2
*Missa solemnis*, op. 132: 32
Piano Concerto no. 1, op. 15: 191, 193
Piano Concerto no. 2, op. 19: 143, 191, 193
Piano Concerto no. 3, op. 37, 191-93
Piano Concerto no. 4, op. 58
    Articulation (*cantabile*, staccato, pizzicato, etc.): 25, 59, 64, 88, 94, 115-16, 141
    Autobiographical associations: 150, 152, 176
    Cadenzas: 94-99, 102-03, 141, 193
    Composition: 1, 4, 52-53
    Continuo writing: 48
    Coda (III): 114, 129-46
    Dynamic markings: 26, 30, 57, 60, 66, 70, 72, 75, 79, 81-84, 87, 91, 115, 119-21, 126, 129-30, 143, 147-48, 193
    Form (irregularities): 48, 56, 82, 91, 114-15, 124, 126, 129
    Generative movement: 25, 52-53
    Harmonic gestures: 57, 70, 72, 75, 80-83, 84, 103, 130, 146
    Imitative polyphony: 126
    Influence of Érard piano: 50-51, 121, 139
    Inspired by Orpheus in Hades: See esp. Ch. 2 and also 190-94
    Inspired by Schiller's "Der neue Orpheus": 194
    Interaction of piano with orchestra: 48, 59, 72, 81, 115
    Intervallic gestures: 64, 72, 77, 83, 87, 89

"Jove" (short-short-short-long) motive: 60, 72, 75, 82, 94-95, 97-98, 103, 169
Length of second movement: 48
Madrigalist gestures: 66-69, 77, 79
Melodic gestures: 64, 66, 70, 72, 77, 80, 82-83, 96, 115, 124
Morality play (as): 102, 149, 189
Orchestration: 25-26, 48, 84,116, 118-21, 124, 126, 129-30, 135, 143, 148, 192-94
Pedals and pedaling (*una corda*, damper): 39-40, 42, 50, 124, 186, 193-94
Performances (19th-century): 49-50
Phrase lengths (irregular): 26, 28-29, 56-57, 91, 115, 118, 169, 176
Piano writing: 48, 72, 81-82, 88-89, 92-94, 104, 117, 121, 126, 130, 139-43, 146, 190
Performance practices: 191, 192
Premiere (private): 2, 12, 15, 33, 87, 187
Premiere (public): 54-55, 87, 187
Recordings on period instruments: 190-94
Registers of piano writing: 26, 72, 81-82, 88-89, 98-99, 124-26, 130, 139-43, 190
Revisions: 87-88, 146-47, 187
Rhythmic gestures: 79, 130
Rhythmic transformation: 75, 88, 92-97, 116, 148
Sketches: 169
Tempo fluctuations: 25
Tempos: 48, 96, 143
Text overlays on melodies: 79, 126

# Beethoven Subject Index